PRESCHOOL PROGRAMS FOR THE DISADVANTAGED

PRESCHOOL PROGRAMS FOR THE DISADVANTAGED:

Five Experimental Approaches to Early Childhood Education

PROCEEDINGS OF THE FIRST ANNUAL

HYMAN BLUMBERG SYMPOSIUM ON RESEARCH

IN EARLY CHILDHOOD EDUCATION

Edited by Julian C. Stanley

THE JOHNS HOPKINS UNIVERSITY PRESS

BALTIMORE AND LONDON

The Johns Hopkins University Press, Baltimore, Maryland 21218
The Johns Hopkins University Press Ltd., London

Library of Congress Catalog Card Number 70–183040
International Standard Book Number 0–8018–1370–0

CONTENTS

PREFACE

THIS VOLUME resulted from the first annual Hyman Blumberg Symposium on Research in Early Childhood Education, which was held at The Johns Hopkins University in February of 1971. Five leading pioneers in the development and evaluation of approaches to educating disadvantaged preschoolers presented papers. Each paper was discussed for at least an hour by from twelve to twenty specialists in preschool education. Three of the discussants reported their reactions to the speeches and discussion. Revised versions of the eight papers appear herein.

On February 1, the symposium began when President Lincoln Gordon of The Johns Hopkins University welcomed to the campus the audience of some 800 persons from all over the country. Mr. Sam Nocella, International Vice President of the Amalgamated Clothing Workers of America (ACWA), which had provided the $110,000 endowment, the income from which finances the Blumberg symposia, introduced a number of ACWA guests, and Mr. Jacob Potofsky, General President of ACWA, inaugurated the symposium on behalf of the union.

The keynote address was then given by congressional representative Patsy Mink of Hawaii, who is a leader in child-care legislation.

Although the ACWA has no responsibility for the papers and discussions at the Blumberg symposia, it is vitally interested in child day care centers for the children of working mothers and is cooperating generously with The Johns Hopkins University in making physical arrangements for the symposia. Special thanks are due Sam Nocella, Howard D.

Samuel, Melvin Bourne, and Lowman G. Daniels for this assistance.

The discussant group consisted of the five speakers and Mary D. S. Ainsworth, Thelma L. Baldwin, Harry Beilin, Courtney B. Cazden, Lowman G. Daniels, Alan J. FitzPatrick, Edith W. King, Jean Orost, Julian C. Stanley, R. H. Starr, Jr., and Roger A. Webb.

The suggestions for the conduct and content of future meetings by those who attended this one are helping us plan the next Blumberg symposium for March 31–April 1, 1972.

Hyman Blumberg, whom the symposia honor, was Executive Vice President of the Amalgamated Clothing Workers of America. He died several years ago, but his son, Professor Phillip I. Blumberg of the Boston University School of Law, was present to join with us in honoring his distinguished father with this permanent memorial to his leadership and to unique collaboration of labor with a major university.

Although the papers differ considerably in content and style, they have a common theme: improving the educational readiness of preschoolers from environments that do not provide the cognitive stimulation most middle-class children receive early in life. Carl Bereiter, David Weikart, and Oralie McAfee approach this objective directly, via special curricula they have developed and tried out. Mrs. McAfee's program differs from the other two in that it has been employed chiefly with youngsters of Mexican–American, Mexican, and Spanish backgrounds.

Todd Risley's experience with classroom-management and behavioral-conditioning techniques is probably not known to most preschool educators, so it importantly supplements more familiar approaches.

Marion Blank is concerned with personality factors that interfere with learning in school. As she indicates, her methods are one-to-one tutorial and therefore not directly applicable in the usual classroom, but the insights and techniques she provides can be helpful to both therapists and teachers.

The critiques by Harry Beilin, Lowman Daniels, and Courtney Cazden interrelate, place in perspective, and extend the contents of the five papers.

We are indebted to the eight authors for making these contributions in a crucially important area—the cognitive facilitation of culturally disadvantaged preschoolers.

Rose Stanley prepared the index of names and helped in numerous other ways, and I am glad to have had at hand the talents of Nancy Middleton Gallienne of The Johns Hopkins University Press.

JULIAN C. STANLEY
Department of Psychology
The Johns Hopkins University

PRESCHOOL PROGRAMS FOR THE DISADVANTAGED

CARL BEREITER
The Ontario Institute for Studies in Education
Toronto, Ontario, Canada

I · AN ACADEMIC PRESCHOOL FOR DISADVANTAGED CHILDREN: CONCLUSIONS FROM EVALUATION STUDIES

I SHALL SET FORTH here some generalizations about preschool education, based on evaluative research that has been done on the academic preschool for disadvantaged children, more familiarly known as the Bereiter–Engelmann program. To base general conclusions on what is essentially product-testing research is, of course, a highly speculative if not fanciful undertaking. There is no true separation of variables in product-testing research, only the single variable of product entity, and so it is difficult to defend any generalization beyond the products tested. Nevertheless, I think the effort is worth making for two reasons. The first is that there is not much else besides product testing research to base inferences on when it comes to questions of what leads to what in preschool education. There are the careful studies of Carolyn Stern and Evan Keislar that investigate, for instance, the conditions under which verbalization does or does not facilitate learning in young children; but these studies stand largely alone. For the rest, we have either program evaluations that do not separate variables or laboratory experiments that are remote enough from real-life learning so that inferences from them are equally speculative.

Another reason for trying to draw inferences from product-testing research is that unless such general inferences can be drawn the research will have been largely in vain, since the

1

products themselves change from one study to another and tend to be obsolete by the time the testing is completed—certainly by the time that long-term effects have been evaluated. Thus, in the case of the Bereiter–Engelmann program, the target of evaluation studies has never actually been the program as set forth in the 1966 book, *Teaching Disadvantaged Children in the Preschool,* but rather local modifications or subsequent revisions of it. And also the original program has since been superseded by the DISTAR program of Engelmann and others, the Conceptual Skills Program of Bereiter and others, and, most recently, the Open Court Kindergarten Program of Bereiter and Hughes, all of which differ from one another and from the original program on practically any dimension one might name. Thus even a simple statement of product evaluation requires judgments about what factors in a given program are central and about the extent to which these factors have been controlled.

Unfortunately, evaluation studies of preschool programs have with few exceptions compared a single program with a control condition, the control condition usually involving no treatment. Such studies, even when adequately designed to test treatment effects, allow only the most tenuous comparisons between one program and another, because each program is evaluated by a different experiment conducted in a different location with a different population, different testers, and so on.

There have, however, been several studies in which the Bereiter–Engelmann program has been compared with other programs or types of preschool education, using experimental procedures designed to maximize comparability of results for the various treatments. These studies, on which the remainder of this discussion will be based, are described here briefly.

1. *The Illinois study* (Karnes et al. 1969) was primarily concerned with comparison of the Ameliorative program originated by Karnes, the Bereiter–Engelmann program (called "Direct Verbal" in that study), and a Traditional program. However, related experiments evaluated a Montessori program and a treatment which merely involved placing disadvantaged

children in various private nursery schools. Subjects for all the comparison groups were drawn by stratified random sampling from a common pool of children in Urbana–Champaign, Illinois, meeting Head Start eligibility criteria. Stratification was by three levels of Binet IQ, and the children were between four and five years of age as of December 1 of the school year. All groups were tested by the same testers, although a blind procedure was not employed. It should be noted that this study, like most other preschool evaluation studies but unlike the studies to be described below, was a "home ball park" evaluation. That is to say, the Ameliorative and Direct Verbal treatments were carried out by the staffs that developed them.

2. *The Kalamazoo study* (Erickson et al. 1969) compared Bereiter–Engelmann, traditional (called "Enrichment" in that study), and no-treatment control groups drawn from a common pool of Head Start-eligible four-year-olds by stratified random sampling according to geographical area. A novel feature of the evaluation was the employment of a cross-over design whereby the samples of children who had been in the two experimental preschool programs were each divided into two groups, one of which continued with the same treatment in kindergarten and one crossed over to the other treatment. Testing on the Stanford–Binet, the main dependent variable of the study, was blind.

3. *Ypsilanti Preschool Demonstration Project* (Weikart 1972) compares the Cognitively Oriented curriculum developed at Ypsilanti, the Bereiter–Engelmann program (called "Language Training" in that study), and a traditional program (called "Unit-Based curriculum"). Subjects were randomly assigned to treatment from among three-year-old black children identified as functionally mentally retarded (low IQ but no discoverable organic impairment).

4. *The Louisville study* (Miller and Dyer 1970) compared Bereiter–Engelmann; the DARCEE program, developed at the George Peabody College for Teachers by Gray and Klaus (1968); Montessori; and Traditional. Over two hundred four-year-olds, almost all black, were involved in these experimental

treatments. The design was not completely randomized, there being ten schools involved, with enough children for at most two different experimental treatments. This study included an extensive investigation of process variables as well as effect variables. Testing was carried out blind and with balancing to control effects of tester differences.

5. *The New York State study* (Di Lorenzo et al. 1969). Eight different preschool programs, each conducted in a different community, were included in this study. In effect there were eight separate experiments of the single treatment-versus-control group design, but the standardization of evaluation procedures and the centralized monitoring of program characteristics allows for somewhat more comparability than would be obtained from unrelated experiments. The most clearly identifiable treatments were the Bereiter–Engelmann, adaptations of which were used in two communities, and the Montessori, which was used in one. One other community used a structured approach with cognitive emphasis, and the rest could be classed as traditional.

In describing the above studies, I have not indicated sample sizes, since they are a rather complex matter in every case. However, the size of the several studies can be approximated from the number of children in the Bereiter–Engelmann treatments of each study for whom end-of-preschool IQ scores were reported. The numbers are 29 for the Illinois study, 136 for the Kalamazoo study, 25 for the Ypsilanti study, 64 for the Louisville study, and 69 for the New York State study. The other experimental groups used in these studies were generally of similar size.

The fact that a number of independent researchers have chosen to deal with the Bereiter–Engelmann program in their investigations is easy to explain plausibly. It is not, I think, that they have found the program intrinsically interesting or appealing, but that they have seen it as representing an extreme on a dimension that they wished to study. As Erickson et al. (1969) put it, the program is "at the heart of one of the most burning issues in nursery school education today, namely, open-ended enrichment programs versus highly structured, detailed methods of instruction" (p. 3). If the issue is drawn as Erickson has stated it, then I think there would be little disagreement that the Bereiter–Engelmann program stands as the most extreme and clear-cut version of a "highly structured, detailed method of instruction."

I would, however, call special attention to the term "instruction." There are other highly structured programs and there are other detailed methods, but in no other preschool program, to my knowledge, are the instructional goals quite so clear-cut nor the procedures so exclusively devoted to achieving those goals in the most efficient manner. Although certain features of the program, such as pattern drill and the rapid pace of teaching, attract notice, I would assert that the program is not bound or distinguished by any particular methods, but is at bottom distinguished entirely by the degree to which content and method are combined into a fully engineered instructional program.

Accordingly, the kinds of general inferences that can be drawn from evaluations of the Bereiter–Engelmann program are likely to be inferences about the value of deliberate instruction at the preschool level. The remainder of this paper is devoted to the discussions of three general conclusions related to this issue.

1. *The Bereiter–Engelmann program has clearly had more impact on IQ and achievement than the traditional, child-centered approach, but not necessarily more impact than other programs with a strong instructional emphasis.* This conclusion has been borne out consistently by all the studies mentioned above. This is also the conclusion arrived at by Bissell (1970) in her reanalysis of data from the Illinois, Ypsilanti, and New York State studies. The results have been replicated widely enough and with a great enough variety of cognitive and achievement measures so that there is no serious problem in generalizing the conclusion to diverse populations of disadvantaged children or to diverse measures. The problem rather is to decide to what kinds of treatments the conclusions

can be generalized: what are the limits of the categories, *traditional, child-centered approach, and programs with a strong instructional emphasis*?

I have elsewhere (Bereiter 1970) discussed the common body of cognitive content that seems to be found in preschool programs of all types: identification of colors, shapes, numbers, letters, materials, parts of objects, uses, and actions, and the use of prepositions, comparisons, categories, and logical operators. This content has been dealt with in traditional preschool materials and activities and figures prominently in intelligence tests for young children. By programs with a strong instructional emphasis I mean ones in which the teacher's activities are specifically geared toward seeing to it that every child masters this content. In the traditional or child-centered approach the teacher's activities may be intended to promote learning of this content, but the teacher is not held responsible for seeing that the learning actually occurs.

Among the programs that emphasize instruction, there are conspicuous differences in method and less conspicuous ones in content. Some investigators have also tried to distinguish them on the basis of broad goals, but in the absence of observational evidence to the contrary, I regard such distinctions as purely rhetorical. Bissell (1970), for instance, distinguishes a structured-cognitive approach, exemplified by the Ameliorative program of Karnes, and a structured-informational program, exemplified by the Bereiter–Engelmann program—the former emphasizing cognitive processes and the latter supposedly ignoring these and concentrating upon "correct" responses. I observed these two programs operating side by side for two years and, while I could detect many differences in method and organization, I did not observe anything to support the distinction Bissell has made. Such distinctions derive, apparently, entirely from the kinds of theoretical ornamentation that program originators use to raise the tone of their reports.

This is not to say that the instructional programs are identical in effect. In comparison with other instructional programs, the Bereiter–Engelmann program has tended to show higher immediate IQ gains on the Stanford–Binet (Miller and Dyer 1970; Karnes et al. 1969; Weikart 1972). The Karnes program has shown higher gains in reading readiness, the DARCEE program on Peabody Picture Vocabulary. These differences can be plausibly explained by differences in content emphasis. The Bereiter–Engelmann program contains relatively little work on vocabulary development or paper-and-pencil exercises of the kind used in readiness testing, but does entail more verbal reasoning and problem solving.

Having noted that different instructional programs appear to teach somewhat different things, we need not analyze the differences any further, as if to tease out all the differences and then weigh them up to decide which program offers the most of what. Such comparisons may be worth while if one is shopping for a program to install, but they are not instructive because there is very little evidence that learning one thing does more good than learning another. Gains on predictor variables are not necessarily predictive of gains on the criterion, as shown in studies of alphabet learning. Among preschool children, knowledge of the alphabet is a good predictor of future reading success, yet training in letter names did not transfer to subsequent reading achievement, although training in letter sounds did (Johnson 1970; Samuels 1970).

It would be helpful to have similar evidence on the relative value of vocabulary building versus training in the more precise and flexible use of words already known—on the transfer value, that is, of such learning to worthwhile tasks like reading. Merely to know that one kind of teaching yields better scores on a vocabulary test and the other on the Basic Concept Inventory is not much help. It is not known whether gains on these tests or on general intelligence or readiness tests are of any value.

From the data available on transfer of preschool treatment to later school learning, we have no grounds for distinguishing between programs with strong instructional emphasis. Again, they do better than the traditional, child-centered programs (Bissell 1970), but they do not differ noticeably from one another. Comparative data on transfer effects are much more scanty than on immediate effects, however. The only strictly comparable follow-up data are those for the Karnes and Bereiter–Engelmann programs (Karnes et al. 1969), where no differences in subsequent achievement appear, although both show achievement in first and second grades superior to that obtained with children in a traditional program.

One seemingly implausible conclusion that may be drawn from the studies to date is that all programs that have set out in a deliberate fashion to teach the core content of preschool education have succeeded, no matter how they have gone about it. The conclusion is probably not true, in that the programs under consideration here are ones that had enough success to have enjoyed continued funding for long enough to carry out extended evaluations and to have been investigated by researchers interested in comparative evaluation. On the other hand, I think it is reasonable to say that the core content mentioned earlier, consisting largely of everyday concepts, is not very hard to teach. It is not like phonics or fractions where, if the teacher is not careful, she can muddle the children's minds so that they not only don't learn it but they are rendered to some extent incapable of learning it thereafter. From this standpoint it may be said that the differences in *method* represented in the various instructional programs have not been put to adequate test. They would need to be applied to the teaching of something difficult. Reading and arithmetic have been taught in the Bereiter–Engelmann program. These are hard to teach, and they were taught with success: children at the end of kindergarten were averaging second-grade level in word recognition and in arithmetic computation (Bereiter 1968). Since the other programs have not tried to teach anything this difficult to children so young, there is no evidence to say they couldn't do it. I have only my own experience to go on in saying that I do not think that the more casual, unprogrammed kinds of instruction that characterize programs other than Bereiter–Engelmann are equal to the task of teaching anything difficult.

Special note must be taken of the showing made by Montessori classes. Three of the studies mentioned thus far included

Montessori classes among the treatments compared (Di Lorenzo 1969; Karnes 1969; Miller and Dyer 1971). In all of these the Montessori classes produced results similar to those of traditional classes and thus inferior to those that I have been calling instructional approaches. In a study involving middle-class children (Bereiter 1966), Montessori-trained four-year-olds lagged far behind Bereiter–Engelmann-trained four-year-olds in reading, arithmetic, and spelling, although not in psycholinguistic skills. The Montessori method is so unusual, of course, that it is going to make a strange bedfellow no matter what category of program it is put into. Bissell (1970) labels it a "structured-environment" approach and puts it into a category with the "New Nursery School" of Nimnicht and Meier. Such a designation is reasonable, but doesn't take account of the very elaborate and systematic pedagogy of sense training and concept teaching which the Montessori method prescribes.

One source of difficulty in describing the Montessori program is that it is sequential, the infant program containing activities appropriate for children from three to five years or older. It is the higher-level activities, involving work with letters, numbers, and science concepts, that have drawn attention to the Montessori method as a possible vehicle for cognitive enrichment and acceleration, but it is entirely possible that disadvantaged preschool children, brought in for one year of Montessori schooling, never work their way up to these activities. The lower-level activities, which center upon housekeeping skills and sense training, are not ones that would be expected to produce noteworthy cognitive gains. As for the higher-level activities, they differ from those in most instructional programs in being strictly tied to a few concrete representations of concepts. As Mussen, Conger, and Kagan (1969, pp. 432–33) point out, such a method tends to produce failure to abstract in young children.

2. *The "traditional" nursery-school and kindergarten program is not a serious contender as an educational program.* Not only has the "traditional" approach failed to achieve as good results in cognitive learning as the more instructional

approaches, it has failed to demonstrate any redeeming advantages. In the Kalamazoo and Louisville studies a variety of motivation and adjustment measures were taken: in the Kalamazoo study, teacher ratings of adjustment, observer tabulations of deviancies, and records of attendance; in the Louisville study, ratings by teachers, ratings by testers, and scores on the Cincinnati Autonomy Battery. On none of these indicators did the traditionally taught children show themselves to be better off than those in the more instructional programs. In the Kalamazoo study they were significantly lower, although superior to controls.

One of the cleanest sets of results is from the Kalamazoo study's analysis of kindergarten attendance records. Here children who had been in a Bereiter–Engelmann preschool showed higher kindergarten attendance than those who had been in a traditional preschool, who in turn showed higher attendance than those who had not been to any preschool. But within each of these three groups, those who attended a Bereiter–Engelmann kindergarten showed higher attendance than those who attended a regular kindergarten. Now it is not at all clear what child characteristics attendance is an indicator of; but the same may be said of any other available measure of childhood personality and adjustment, impressive test labels notwithstanding. One thing that can be said of attendance that cannot be said confidently of test variables is that it must indicate something important and not some trivial instrument factor. School attendance would seem to be a social indicator, a very gross index of how well things are going with a child in relation to school. Its very lack of specificity guards it from the complaint that can be made against other variables in the evaluation of preschool effects—that they do not do justice to the broad socio-emotional goals of a child-centered program. I do not know any way to interpret a difference in school attendance in favor of children in the Bereiter–Engelmann program that is not damaging to the claims made for the traditional child-centered program.

Experimenters who have used a traditional program as one kind of treatment have all evidenced difficulty in defining what such a program is. The name itself, of course, isn't descriptive of what goes on and is regarded by many early childhood educators as pejorative. Yet even to find a name that distinguishes it from competing programs is difficult. Early childhood educators have also complained to me that there is no such thing as a traditional program or a "regular" Head Start approach, that they differ widely. Such differences, however, have always escaped my observation and apparently they also escape detection by systematic classroom observation. (Lois-ellin Datta [private communication] reports that efforts to study the effects of natural variations among Head Start programs have had little success because there simply was not enough variation to work with.)

Miller and Dyer, in the Louisville study, offered a systematic point-by-point comparison of the four types of programs they studied. The traditional approach, interestingly enough, is largely distinguished from the rest on the basis of things that are not done. The video-tape monitoring of teacher behavior in the same study provides striking support for the ideological distinction. Teachers in the traditional program are not so much distinguished by differences in the relative frequency of different kinds of teaching acts (as are teachers in the other three programs) as by the generally low frequency of teaching acts of any kind. The mean frequency of teaching acts of any kind among the traditional teachers is less than half that of teachers in the Bereiter–Engelmann classes (Miller and Dyer 1970, p. 53).

Furthermore, the only categories of behavior in which traditional teachers showed up as noticeably more active than teachers in the other programs were Contingent Negative Verbal Reinforcement, Conduct Modification, and Academic-Verbal Giving (lecturing).

The picture that emerges from these results is one that accords with my own observations. It is that the traditional approach does not represent a *different* way of teaching from those represented in newer programs but simply represents a lower order of program, one that is more custodial and less purposefully educational. The lesser overall amount of teaching behavior and the greater emphasis on behavior management suggest the custodial function. The greater use of straight verbal presentation as a way of giving information is entirely out of keeping with traditional doctrine if it is taken to indicate deliberate pedagogical method. It is quite understandable, however, on the assumption that instruction occurs only incidentally in traditional classrooms, without prior planning, so that the teacher is not prepared to communicate information in any other way than through just talking. To demonstrate or model a concept, to ask leading questions, to develop a concept through sequenced tasks—any of these require more preparation and a more deliberate intent to teach than is found in the traditional class.

It seems to me somewhat misleading to go on treating the traditional approach as one among a host of alternative approaches to teaching young children. It is better seen, not as a distinctive approach to teaching, but as a system of custodial child care that may incorporate to a greater or lesser extent various educational components similar to those found in instructional programs for young children, but that is primarily distinguished by its minimization of teaching. The true issue between the traditional approach and the various instructional approaches is not *how* young children should be taught but *whether.* This is still a live issue, far from having been settled by research. It is to this issue that I now turn.

3. *The long-term effects of preschool instruction are about as good as can be expected.* However impressive the immediate results of preschool compensatory instruction may be, and however much encouragement may be drawn from follow-up achievement data, the fact remains that no preschool program shows any promise of making, by itself, any *permanent* difference in the scholastic success of poor children.

The standard against which long-term results of preschool intervention are judged seems to be that of the Skeels (1966) experiment, where thirty years later the experimental subjects were leading successful lives and the control subjects were in miserable shape. This is a very unfair standard, however, for the Skeels intervention (taking children out of an institution and putting them in foster homes) was not only much more extreme, but it was an intervention that continued life long. Would anyone expect that putting children into foster homes at age five for one year and then sending them back to the institution would show such effects thirty years later? To me it is quite remarkable that some preschool interventions are showing statistically significant effects for three years or more after the cessation of treatment. It is also noteworthy that these programs are the same kinds of instructional programs that produce the greatest immediate results.

To treat the eventual vanishing of preschool effects as failure is to imply either that preschool compensatory education is futile or that the effective method has yet to be discovered. Either of these conclusions *could* be true, but those who think they follow from current evidence are applying criteria of success to preschool education that are not applied in any other realm of human effort. They are asking the doctor for a pill they can take when they are ten that will prevent them from getting fat when they are fifty.

Reason would have it that if we have designed a preschool program that produces benefits lasting for three years, then instead of agonizing that they didn't last for five or ten, we should be concerned with what can be done in the years after preschool to produce further benefits. This, of course, is a popular notion, one that lies behind the entire Follow-Through program. It raises, however, some troubling questions concerning preschool education.

a. If it is granted that education for poor children must be improved over the whole span of school years, then is it any longer necessary or practical to invest heavily in preschool education for such children? In other words, is preschool education anything more than the stone in the stone soup?

b. Is there justification for heavy investment in a continued search for more effective methods of preschool education, or have the limits of effectiveness largely been reached?

Both of these are policy questions that have to be acted upon whether there is any pertinent evidence or not, and so whatever faintly valid evidence may be dredged out of evaluation studies is that much to the good.

The cross-over data from the Kalamazoo study afford some

evidence that is directly pertinent to the first question. Put more crudely, the first question reads: If you are going to follow up anyway, does it make any difference what you follow up on? The Kalamazoo study found that children in regular kindergarten classes did better if they had been in a Bereiter–Engelmann preschool than if they had been in a traditional one, or had had no preschool at all. On the other hand, children from these three preschool conditions who went into a Bereiter–Engelmann kindergarten all ended up at about the same level of performance. If the Bereiter–Engelmann kindergarten is taken to represent follow-up—that is, the continuation of special treatment—then it would appear that it does not make much difference what one follows up on: the preschool treatments could have been eliminated without loss. On the other hand, when there was no follow-up—that is, when children were put into a regular kindergarten program —performance was highly dependent on the nature of preschool experiences.

This finding is pregnant with implications. Consider, for instance, how the results might have been interpreted if all the children from the three preschool conditions had gone into a Bereiter–Engelmann kindergarten, and if this kindergarten program had somehow gotten itself established as normal, so that no mention was made of what kind of kindergarten program it was. Then the data would have shown that preschool effects "washed out" when the children got to kindergarten. One might even have been tempted to blame the kindergarten for washing out those grand effects. Under the actual circumstances, however, with traditional kindergarten classes for comparison, it appears that the washing out of effects was a good thing, since it consisted of bringing those children with the less favorable preschool experience up to the level of those with the more favorable experience.

A rather more complex set of results from recent phases of the Louisville study (Miller and Dyer 1971; Miller et al. 1971) appears to support the same interpretation of "wash out." After completing the preschool treatments described previously, children were branched into either a regular kindergarten or into a Follow-Through kindergarten program described as "a highly academic, individualized program structured as a token-economy" (Miller and Dyer 1971, p. 4). Children who received the Follow-Through treatment did significantly better than those who went to regular kindergarten, regardless of their preschool experience. There was also a clear wash-out of differences in the Follow-Through treatment, with children who had received no preschool education and those who had received a traditional one scoring as well as those who had received the more effective experimental treatments. On the other hand, in the regular kindergarten there were significant differences due to preschool experience. However, in contrast to the Kalamazoo findings, the differences were by no means a simple carry-over of differences observed at the end of preschool. On one of the main measures, the Metropolitan Readiness Test, the lowest scores were obtained by regular kindergarten children who had had Bereiter–Engelmann preschool. A number of other shifts in relative standing are puzzling as to what kinds of interactions with preschool experience actually took place in the regular kindergarten classrooms of this study; but the overall result, that an effective instructional program in kindergarten can wash out preschool differences in a favorable way while a conventional kindergarten does not do so, remains consistent with the Kalamazoo findings.

Extrapolated, these results would suggest that a highly effective program at any level of schooling will overcome the effects of variations in educational experience up to that level. The suggestion is probably not true, of course. If it were we could concentrate all our efforts on making a bang-up success of the last year of schooling and not worry about whether children learned anything in the years preceding. But so long as it appears true that an effective kindergarten program will overcome differences in preschool experience, we must question the wisdom of concentrating compensatory education on the preschool period.

The wise strategy for the present would seem to be to look for elementary school programs that are more successful than the present ones at washing out the effects of differences in earlier school experience. This strategy does not, however, preclude the continued search for more effective methods of preschool education. On this matter we have to ask ourselves what increased effects we would want or have any reason to expect were possible.

Such a question invites visionary responses à la George Leonard (1966). Generalizing from what we have been able to teach in our experimental programs, however, I am inclined toward the more pedestrian position that existing technology already enables us to teach young children far more than they can benefit from. What we need to do is not discover ways to teach them more but rather construct articulated educational programs that permit us to teach in the preschool what will be of use later and to teach later what builds upon what was learned in the preschool.

Thus I do not believe we need to be devoting resources to developing a better preschool program because we are in no position to say what a preschool program ought to accomplish that present ones do not. As we noted previously, the various effective instructional programs do not accomplish precisely the same things, but there is no basis for saying that the accomplishment of one is more valuable than that of another. I think, therefore, that we are at a point where development of preschool programs, if it is to proceed any further, has to be joined to elementary school curriculum design. The two questions: "What does a child need to know in order to be ready for first grade?" and "What does a child need to know in order to get the most out of being four years old?" have about yielded their all. The first has yielded the core content of preschool education mentioned previously and the second has yielded such things as handling a paint brush and putting on a coat (to mention only objectives that can be acted on; the second question also gives rise to an abundance of fine sentiments). Only by joining preschool education with elementary school curriculum can we begin plausibly asking the potentially much more productive question: "What things can we teach a child of four and five that can then be built upon in the first grade and after?"

My attitude toward the failure of preschool programs to produce lasting gains is perhaps cavalier. I realize that the more accepted behavior, which I have on occasions engaged in myself, is to express sincere regrets that things haven't turned out better and then offer an explanation which, while vague and speculative, makes it clear that I am not at fault. It is also possible to find cause for optimism in follow-up results. Verbal reports from Karnes and Erickson indicate that Bereiter–Engelmann children continue to show achievement advantages over control and traditionally taught children as far as the third grade. Weikart children, from his original experimental treatment, show achievement advantages as late as sixth grade. To me, however, the most parsimonious hypothesis to account for these persisting advantages is that there was a degree of continuing differential treatment given to experimental group children—by virtue of their being assigned to different streams on entry into regular school. I know this to have been the case in the Illinois study, where the schools used IQ and other scores from the research testing to place children in first grade streams. Differential treatment in the Ypsilanti study may have been even more marked, judging from Weikart's verbal report of a substantially larger proportion of control group children being assigned to special classes for the mentally retarded.

The data on long-term effects of preschool intervention are disillusioning but not, to me at least, discouraging. The illusion that they serve to dispel is that there is some magic in the early years of intellectual development, such that a little difference there will make a lot of difference later. What we seem to be finding instead is that a lot of difference there may just possibly make a little difference later. Weakening of the "magic years" illusion will, I hope, render more credible the position that Engelmann and I have argued from the beginning, that learning in young children is just learning: some things can be taught to young children and some cannot; some of the things that can be taught will prove useful later and some will not; what will prove useful later is not determined by some innate chain of development but by the actual course of real-life events. The corollary that I have argued in this section is that one way to make preschool learning more use-ful is to alter the actual course of subsequent school events so as to make use of it.

IMPLICATIONS FOR DAY CARE AND FOR EARLY CHILDHOOD EDUCATION RESEARCH

Because of the twin concerns of the Hyman Blumberg Me-morial Symposium with the providing of day care services for children of working parents and with research in early child-hood education, it seems appropriate to comment specifically on the implications that the foregoing conclusions have for these two concerns.

With respect to day care I am an outsider, and I make the following observations without pretending to know the com-plexities of the enterprise. It appears that the main thing wrong with day care is that there is not enough of it, and the main reason there is not enough of it is that it costs too much. At the same time, those who are professionally dedicated to advancing day care seem to be pressing continually to make it more costly by setting certification requirements for day care workers and by insisting that day care should be educa-tional and not just high-quality institutionalized baby-sitting.

What the previous discussion should suggest is that pro-ducing a measurable educational effect in young children is far from easy, that it requires as serious a commitment to cur-riculum and teaching as does education in older children. I cannot imagine day care centers on a mass basis carrying out educational programs of the kind needed to produce measur-able effect. If they cannot do so, then it will prove in the long run a tactical blunder to keep insisting that day care must be educational. Sooner or later those who pay for it will begin demanding to see evidence that educational benefits are being produced, and there will be no evidence.

It would seem to me much wiser to seek no more from day care than the sort of high-quality custodial care that a child would receive in a well-run home, and to seek ways to achieve this level of care at a cost that would make it reasonable to provide for all those who need it. One should not have to justify day care on the grounds that it will make children do better in school, any more than one should seek such justification for a hot lunch program. A child has a right to a square meal regardless of whether or not it helps him read better.

A well-run and well-equipped day care center resembles very closely a traditional preschool—which I have argued is also primarily custodial in its function. The traditional preschool has managed to flourish, with its clientele of upper-middle-class families willing to pay, without having to promise educational benefits. It has earned a place for itself simply by providing a wholesome experience for children in pleasant surroundings and in the company of other children. I do not see why day care centers should have to promise more in order to justify their existence.

Early childhood education has been a thriving area of research and development during the past five years. High expectations and availability of money combined to draw talented investigators into the area. Both the expectations and the money are likely to diminish and with them, no doubt, the special attractiveness of the field. The likely result, however, is that early childhood education research will merge more with educational research in general. There is much to be done in the early childhood field, for instance in the discovery of the critical variables in instructional treatment and in the closer analysis of particular learning problems; but there is no reason why such research should stand apart from the main body of research into classroom learning. Abandonment of the "magic years" illusion should have, in the long run, beneficial effects on research as well as on educational practice.

REFERENCES

Bereiter, C. 1966. *Acceleration of intellectual development in early childhood.* Washington, D.C.: U.S. Office of Education.

———. 1968. A nonpsychological approach to early compensatory education. Pp. 337–46 in M. Deutsch et al. (eds.), *Social class, race, and psychological development.* New York: Holt, Rinehart & Winston.

———. 1970. Designing programs for classroom use. Pp. 204–7 in F. F. Korten et al. (eds.), *Psychology and the problems of society.* Washington, D.C.: American Psychological Association.

Bereiter, C., and Engelmann, S. 1966. *Teaching disadvantaged children in the preschool.* Engelwood Cliffs, N.J.: Prentice-Hall.

Bissell, J. S. 1970. *The cognitive effects of pre-school programs for disadvantaged children.* Bethesda, Maryland: National Institute of Child Health and Human Development, June 1970 (mimeographed).

Di Lorenzo, L., Salter, R., and Brady, J. J. 1969. *Prekindergarten programs for educationally disadvantaged children.* Washington, D.C.: U.S. Office of Education.

Erickson, E. L., McMillan, J., Bennell, J., Hoffman, L., and Callahan, O. D. 1969. *Experiments in Head Start and early education: Curriculum structures and teacher attitudes.* Washington, D.C.: Office of Economic Opportunity, Project Head Start.

Gray, S. W., and Klaus, R. A. 1968. The Early Training Project and its general rationale. Pp. 63–70, in R. D. Hess and R. M. Baer (eds.), *Early Education.* Chicago: Aldine.

Johnson, R. J. 1970. The effect of training in letter names on success in beginning reading for children of differing abilities. Paper presented at annual meeting of the American Educational Research Association, Minneapolis, Minnesota, March 1970.

Karnes, M. B., Hodgins, A. S., Teska, J. A., and Kirk, S. A. 1969. *Research and development program on preschool disadvantaged children.* Vol. I. Washington, D.C.: U.S. Office of Education.

Leonard, G. B. 1968. *Education and ecstacy.* New York: Delacorte Press.

Miller, L. B., and Dyer, J. L. 1970. Experimental variation of Head Start curricula: A comparison of current approaches. Annual progress report, June 1, 1969–May 31, 1970. Louisville, Kentucky: University of Louisville, Department of Psychology.

———. 1971. Two kinds of kindergarten after four types of Head Start. Louisville, Kentucky: University of Louisville, Department of Psychology.

Miller, L. B., et al. 1971. Experimental variation of Head Start curricula: A comparison of current approaches. Progress Report No. 9, March 1, 1971–May 31, 1971. Louisville, Kentucky: University of Louisville, Department of Psychology.

Mussen, P. H., Conger, J. J., and Kagan, J. 1969. *Child development and personality* (3rd ed.). New York: Harper & Row.

Samuels, S. J. 1970. Letter-name versus letter-sound knowledge as factors influencing learning to read. Paper presented at annual meeting of the American Educational Research Association, Minneapolis, Minnesota, March 1970.

Skeels, H. M. 1966. Adult status of children with contrasting early experiences. *Monograph of the Society for Research in Child Development*, 51, no. 3.

Weikart, D. P. 1972. Relationship of curriculum, teaching, and learning in preschool education. Pp. 22–66, in present volume.

DAVID P. WEIKART
High/Scope Educational Research Foundation
Ypsilanti, Michigan 48197

II · RELATIONSHIP OF CURRICULUM, TEACHING, AND LEARNING IN PRESCHOOL EDUCATION

THE MOST PRESSING PROBLEM facing preschool education as part of the total compensatory education effort is to understand the conditions necessary for the operation of effective preschool education programs. We've come a long way from the early 60's and the simple questions of the preschool's effectiveness in helping disadvantaged children develop social-emotional, cognitive, and language skills for success in later school years. We've also developed beyond the point where endless discussions about whether or not my theory is bigger and stronger than your theory have any meaning. Yet the stage is only now being set for the massive attention that must be given to problems of implementation, if preschool is to have a permanent place in the educational scene and not become another expression of "doing good" for children—an elaborate Christmas-basket approach to education that has been typical of philanthropic efforts in the field of social services.

The transition to this new stage is not complete, and there is still considerable debate about the direction in which research efforts should go. It is difficult to discuss this problem because the field of compensatory preschool education is littered with debris from the battles of the last decade between the ideas of traditional child-development educators and the more modern approaches espoused by educational researchers.

I would like to stand aside from this debate and discuss three basic questions concerning preschool education, using information derived from our research of the last eight years. These are: (1) Does preschool education make a significant difference in the later school performance of disadvantaged children? (2) If preschool education does make a difference, does it matter which curriculum theory or method is employed? and (3) How can we guarantee effective preschool education?

DOES PRESCHOOL EDUCATION MAKE A DIFFERENCE?

From many points of view, to ask that preschool education demonstrate effectiveness as treatment is unusual, for we seldom ask this type of question about educational efforts; certainly it is difficult to find out. For example, while a number of states have adopted statewide kindergarten programs, one seldom hears of comparison studies of achievement rates between those children who went to kindergarten and those who did not. Some school systems have omitted certain grades, having all children skip from, say, the seventh to the ninth grade. Achievement differences between high school graduates of such systems and graduates who have had the "benefit" of an eighth grade are seldom reported. Yet the question whether preschool education makes a difference has been the subject of much debate. For example, the demand that preschool education make an impact on later performance is the major issue in the current criticism of Head Start, and it is the major research focus of the Head Start Planned Variation Study being conducted by the Office of Child Development. What will be the evidence upon which to judge the impact of preschool experience? Will scores from standardized intelligence and achievement tests be used? Or perhaps scores from measures of creativity or problem solving? How about indices of changed attitudes toward education and society in general, or of beneficial effects on younger brothers and sisters? The lack of agreement on criteria is a major stumbling block to answering questions about the impact of preschool education. If, however, the criterion of scores on standardized tests is employed, a partial answer to the question of preschool effectiveness can be found in the research of the past decade.

A number of writers have presented reviews of the early history of the preschool movement. The contributions of such early educators as Comenius, Froebel, Oberlin, Montessori, and McMillan have been summarized by Brittain (1966), Kraft et al. (1968), and Horowitz and Paden (1970). The main impact of these early educators was to create a climate for the serious consideration of the education of the young. They recognized that the experiences of early childhood form the basis for later learning. They tended to stress the value of play, and they often recommended that children be provided with special environments to develop maximally. Montessori developed a special curriculum, complete with new materials and methods. McMillan labored to make nursery schools a part of the English education system. Oberlin saw early education as a way of curing the world of its ills by teaching his view of utopia.

Reviewers of preschools, before the 1960's wave of compensatory education programs, found that most of the information available was on middle-class children enrolled in laboratory schools or on projects of such limited scope that the data were meaningless. Fuller (1960), Sears and Dowley (1963), and Swift (1964) provided excellent reviews. Swift summarized the literature by saying that although there is no evidence that preschool helps a youngster, there also is no evidence that it harms him (hardly a statement destined to elicit wild optimism about the potential of compensatory education).

There was little concern in these early reviews with the issues that are the focus of current preschool programs for the disadvantaged. For example, few projects listed the cognitive aspects of child development as a goal of their programs. Sears and Dowley (1963) recognized this when they commented: "It is curious that in the stated aims and purposes of the nursery school, intellectual development of the child has been very little considered." The kinds of concerns given attention in the traditional nursery school are quite different from those emphasized in the modern cognitively oriented preschool programs.

On the whole, then, the early reviews summarized information about middle-class children attending college-laboratory and church-affiliated nursery schools and reflected the deep concern of traditional nursery school education with "the achievement by the child of some emotional independence of adults without undue side effects such as anxiety or insecurity" (Sears and Dowley 1963, p. 823). They also reflected a philosophical commitment to the freedom of the nursery school teacher to deal independently and intuitively with her children; this view assumes that there is no need to follow a curriculum based on specific cognitive or language theories. The ideal is the master teacher responding to the "needs" of the children as seen from her vantage point of general knowledge about child development and personal wisdom and experience (Weikart 1970).

Of concern in this paper is information that would indicate whether preschool made a difference in later performance as measured by standardized tests or other clear criteria. Data are available from several studies which have passed beyond the category of immediate results and into a long-term follow-up status. The most complete is that by Skeels (1966), who reported thirty-year follow-up results of an early preschool and adoption study by the Iowa Child Welfare Station. The social and occupational adaptation of the experimental children who eventually went into adoptive homes was impressive when compared to the almost total lack of adjustment on the part of the control children who did not participate in preschool and who remained institutionalized. This finding gives considerable strength to the notion that while the immediate impact of a project may be difficult to ascertain, long-term results may be favorable when the intervention results in a basic improvement in the general environment of the child. Since the youngsters in the control group were unable to leave the state institution and did not have the opportunity to live in a normal environment, the results may be seen as evidence of a contrast between long-continued "normal" and deprived environments.

A second study is by Gray and Klaus (1969). The children in their experimental group attended two or three summers of preschool and had one or two years of weekly home teaching by a trained staff member from the project. In their seven-year follow-up report, they concluded that while there seemed to be definite spreading of their project's impact to other children in the community and to younger siblings, by fourth grade there were no significant achievement differences between control and experimental groups. There was, however, a small statistically significant difference in Stanford–Binet IQ scores in favor of the experimental children. It is a remarkable achievement to have sustained an impact on intellectual development through the seventh year of a study and four years after formal intervention.

Karnes (1969) conducted a curriculum comparison study Two structured curricula (the Ameliorative curriculum, operated by Karnes, and the Direct Verbal curriculum, operated by Bereiter and Engelmann) were compared, and a traditionally oriented nursery program was used for baseline data, instead of a non-treatment control group. At the end of the first grade, there was no difference in Stanford–Binet scores between the children in the two experimental programs on the one hand and those in the traditional group on the other. However, the general academic progress of the children in the two experimental programs was better than that of the children in the traditional program.

The fourth longitudinal project that I wish to discuss is the Ypsilanti Perry Preschool Project (Weikart, Deloria, Lawser, and Wiegerink 1970). While the study is not complete—in that follow-up is still under way, with the oldest children in seventh and the youngest in third grade—enough data are available on the first five years of the project for some tentative statements.

This project was an experiment to assess the longitudinal effects of a two-year preschool program designed to compensate for functional mental retardation found in some children from disadvantaged families. The program consisted of daily cognitively oriented preschool classes accompanied by weekly home-teaching visits. The project was operated from September 1962 to June 1967. The population from which the sample was selected was black and economically disadvantaged. Children were assigned to either an experimental or a control group in an essentially random manner, except that the two groups were matched on socio-economic status and Stanford–Binet scores. Instruments used to evaluate program impact were the Stanford–Binet Tests, the Leiter International Performance Scale, the Peabody Picture Vocabulary Test, the Illinois Test of Psycholinguistic Abilities, the California Achievement Test Battery, several parent-attitude instruments, and teacher ratings of children.

The preschool curriculum that evolved during the five years of the project was derived mainly from Piagetian theory and focused on cognitive objectives (Weikart, Rogers, Adcock, and McClelland 1971). Emphasis was placed on making the curriculum flexible enough for the teacher to gear classroom activities to each child's level of development. Verbal stimulation and interaction, sociodramatic play and the learning of concepts through activity were considered more important than social behavior and other traditional concerns of nursery schools. Weekly afternoon home-teaching visits provided each family with an opportunity for personal contact with the child's teacher. The parents were encouraged to participate in the instruction of their children, the goal being to improve their relationship with school and teachers and to involve them in the educational process. The teacher's child management techniques indirectly suggested to the mother alternative ways of handling children. Group meetings were used to reinforce the changes in parents' views regarding the education of their children.

Five pairs of experimental and control groups were used in five replications of the basic experiment. This technique, referred to as small sample replication, offered two advantages which helped enhance the conclusiveness of the results: first, by using a small sample in each replication, better quality control of the classroom operations could be achieved; second, consistent results from the five independent experiments were far more convincing than a single significant result. Each of the five pairs of experimental and control groups was called a "wave," and given a number from 0 through 4. Waves 0 and 1 started preschool in the fall of 1962. Wave 4, the last wave, began in the fall of 1965 and completed the second year in June 1967. Each new wave of children began at age three and remained in the program for two years.

The general findings from the project are:

1. The children who participated in preschool obtained significantly higher scores on the Stanford–Binet IQ test than the control group children. This superior functioning disappeared by third grade. (See Table II–1 and graph, pp. 58–59.)

2. The children who participated in preschool obtained significantly higher scores on achievement tests in elementary school than the control group children. This difference attained significance in first and third grades. (See Table II–2 and graph pp. 60–61.)

3. The children who participated in preschool received better ratings by elementary school teachers in academic, emotional, and social development than the control group children. This difference continued through third grade.

While there is a range of other important research projects not described here (see, for example, Hodges, McCandless, and Spicker 1967; Di Lorenzo 1968; and Beller 1969), the current compensatory preschool projects all tend to support one specific conclusion: Experimental projects in which researchers have direct control of the curriculum, the operation of the project, and the research design seem to offer potential for immediate positive impact in terms of their stated goals (Weikart 1967; Gray 1969; Horowitz and Paden 1970). Such projects can produce measurable impact on intellectual, academic, and social-emotional growth as long as four years after the preschool intervention. Preschool experience *can* make a difference for disadvantaged children. Unfortunately, I am speaking only of special situations. The findings of Hawkridge et al. (1968), the critical review by Freeman (1970), and the Westinghouse study of Head Start (1969) point up the fragility of this conclusion when applied to the field of preschool education beyond special research projects.

Does It Matter Which Curriculum Is Employed?

Since preschool can make a difference under certain conditions, it is important to know if the wide range of early education curricula has differential impact on children. While it is unlikely that any *particular* program with a given orientation is more effective than any other similarly styled program, it would seem reasonable to assume that general approaches differ significantly in their ability to help preschool children. Before discussing a project designed to examine the differential potential of three major general approaches, I would like to present an organizational scheme for the various preschool models.

Most preschool programs may be placed in one of four categories: Programmed, Open Framework, Child-centered, or Custodial.*

In Figure II–1, each of these program types is related to the way teachers and children in such programs participate and interact, in other words, to the teachers' and children's "roles." If the teacher's predominant role is to *initiate*, she plans lessons, organizes projects, and develops activities; she decides what will be done or directly influences what will be done; she presents materials, programs, and ideas; she guides action and directs the efforts of the children. The initiating, or active, teacher usually follows a specific theoretical position, developing her classroom activities from its tenets or following specific procedures prescribed for her. Indeed, an "initiat-

---

* Of course, any system of categorization is a deliberate simplification of the real world. Categories overlap in practice; many preschool programs are eclectic, mixing parts of various general approaches. These mixed models are to be found usually in situations removed from the requirements of a rigorous research design.

Figure II–1. Preschool Curricula Models

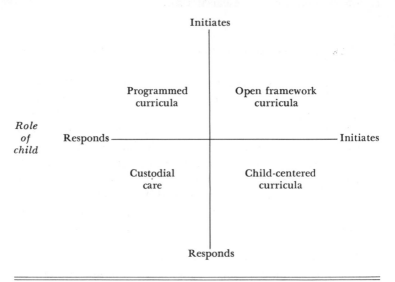

Role of teacher

Initiates

Programmed   Open framework
curricula   curricula

Role
of   Responds ————————————————— Initiates
child

Custodial   Child-centered
care   curricula

Responds

Typical Programs

Programmed curricula: Engelmann–Bereiter's DISTAR
                        Glaser and Resnick's Primary Education

Open framework: Susan Gray's Demonstration and Research
                          Center for Early Education
                        Merle Karnes's Ameliorative Preschool
                        Herbert Sprigle's Learning to Learn
                        David Weikart's Cognitively Oriented

Child-centered: Bank Street College programs
                        Ron Henderson's Tucson Early Education
                          Model
                        Glen Nimnicht's Responsive Environments
                          Program
                        Robert Spaulding's Durham Education
                          Improvement Project
                        Montessori programs

ing teacher" can even be a programmed textbook or a sophisticated computer terminal from which a theory of instruction interpreted by a program developer may be applied through carefully controlled materials. In general, the teacher who initiates is forceful in applying her talents and skills to accomplish specific instructional objectives.

If the teacher's predominant role is to *respond*, she watches the actions of both individual children and groups of children in the classroom environment. She responds to their needs and tries to facilitate their interaction with each other and with the materials in the classroom. While she will introduce materials and activities at specific points, she does this in response to what she feels are the expressed needs of the children. To ascertain these needs, the responding teacher applies the general knowledge of child development she has gained through training and experience. On the whole, the teacher responds carefully through her essentially intuitive understanding of the children's behavior.

When the child *initiates*, he is engaged in direct experience with various objects through manipulation and full use of all his senses; he is involved in role playing and other kinds of fantasy play; and he is active in planning his daily program, determining how he will work in the classroom environment. There is considerable physical movement by the child and a balance among teacher-child, child-child, and child-material interaction patterns. In general the impetus for learning and involvement comes from within the child.

When the child *responds*, he is attentive or receptive; he listens to the teacher and carries out her requests; and he responds verbally to requests and demands. The responding child tends to move about the classroom less than the initiating child, since his predominant role is to wait for and attend to what is prepared and presented to him. In general, this child is working within a clear framework of acceptable behavior and progressing toward a specified goal.

Each of the four preschool types—Programmed, Open Framework, Child-centered, and Custodial—is, among other things, a particular combination of these styles of teacher-child interaction, which will be discussed next.

Programmed. This model combines *teacher initiates* and *child responds*. Several major innovative programs in the current wave of compensatory preschool projects are Programmed curricula. These curricula tend to be directed at clearly defined educational goals, such as the teaching of reading, language skills, and mathematics skills. Although the program developers show little respect for traditional education at any level, the goal of many of these programs is to equip the youngster with the skills necessary to manage the demands of such education. These curricula tend to be rigidly structured, with the teacher dominating the child and with a heavy emphasis on convergent thinking—"Say it the right way"—and learning through repetition and drill. The programs tend to be oriented to specific procedures, equipment, and materials, especially in those approaches that are heavily programmed, with technology ranging from simple language master and tape components to major learning systems with computers and all the trimmings.

The key to the programs in this quadrant is that the curricula are teacher-proof; that is, the curricula are prepared scripts and not subject to extensive modification by the individuals presenting the instructions. As one major exponent of teacher-proof methods said: "If you use my program, 75% of everything you say will be exactly what I tell you to say!" Usually these programs are produced by a central group of program developers and then published or distributed for general use by interested school systems and parent groups. Since these programs assume that everything can be taught by the careful control of the student response, many of them use behavior modification techniques.

The major advantage of the curricula in this quadrant is their ease of distribution to the general field of preschool education, as the performance of the child is keyed to the materials and not to the creative abilities of the teacher. This means that relatively untrained paraprofessionals as well as sophisticated and experienced professionals can effectively use these curricula with little difficulty. In addition, the teacher-proof characteristic appeals to angry parent groups who question the motives or commitment of teachers and who want full teacher accountability for the time their youngsters spend in school. These parents want their children to be taught to read and write and do arithmetic, and these programs do that job without any nonsense. Many school administrators also like these kinds of programs, as they provide effective control of their teaching staff and lend themselves to ordering equipment and supplies in logical units.

Another advantage of Programmed curricula is the ease with which new components may be added as they become necessary or identified. For example, another innovator in the Programmed area was criticized because of the failure of his methods to permit creative experiences for the children. He commented, "If you'll define what you mean by creativity, I'll develop a program to teach it." Then too, these curricula do not make a priori assumptions about the limitations of individual children. The challenge for the teacher is to find out the present limits of the child's knowledge in the area of concern and begin an instructional program to bring him to a well-defined point of competence.

In general, these curricula have clearly defined educational objectives, present a carefully designed and extensive program sequence to move children toward those objectives, and give the teacher explicit instructions as to how to behave during these learning sequences. Teaching is accomplished through the application of scripted materials supplied by the program developers. Learning is seen as the acquisition of correct responses as determined by the materials; anything can be taught to almost any child if the educational goals and behavioral objectives can be specified. The principles which support these programs tend to be drawn from learning theory, behavior management procedures, and language development theory. Examples of this approach are Engelmann Bereiter direct instructional programs such as DISTAR, the Primary Education project of Glaser and Resnick, and language programs such as Carolyn Stern's Preschool Language project.

Open Framework. In this quadrant, representing *teacher initiates–child initiates*, are preschool programs which subscribe to specific theoretical goals, but which depend upon the teacher to create the exact curriculum in which the child participates. These curricula tend to focus upon underlying processes of thinking or cognition and to emphasize that learning comes through direct experience and action by the child. They omit training in specific areas, such as reading or arithmetic, treating these skills as inevitable outcomes of basic cognitive ability. These curricula accept the responsibility of developing the capacity of the child to reason and to recognize the relationship of his own actions to what is happening about him; they tend to be skeptical of claims that solutions to problems or academic skills can be taught directly to preschoolers.

These curricula are usually based upon a theory of child development, the most popular of which is that of Piaget. Using this theory, a curriculum framework is structured so that the teacher has clear guidelines as to how the program should be organized. The curriculum theory delimits the range of preschool activities, giving criteria for judging which activities are appropriate. The framework generally includes directions for structuring the physical environment, arranging and sequencing equipment and materials, and structuring the day. The theory also gives the teacher a framework for organizing her perspectives on the general development of children. It is this open framework that provides discipline to the program.

These curricula tend to be oriented toward organizing and utilizing the *people* involved rather than any special equipment. They demand that the teacher create a transaction between the child and his environment to develop his abilities. And they demand that the child learn by forming concepts through activity, not by repeating what he has been told. The curriculum provides guidelines for establishing these conditions, but does not require special materials or equipment.

One of the major advantages of the Open Framework curricula is that while the teacher must adopt a theoretical position and work within its limits, the specific program she creates is uniquely hers, developed as an expression of her attempt to meet the needs of the children in her group. This personal involvement on the part of the teacher means she becomes deeply committed to her program, and it is highly probable that she will continue to implement her program over a long period of time. At the same time, since the curriculum is based upon a specific theory, her expression of that curriculum can be closely examined by others, who know both the theory and children, to provide the teacher with guidance and assistance, facilitating quality control of the program.

Another advantage of Open Framework curricula is that since the programs focus on the development of basic cognitive processes rather than on social-emotional growth, and since the specific curriculum is created by the teacher by carefully planning activities according to the developmental levels of individual children, they are relatively free of cultural bias and untested assumptions about children's abilities. Thus they can be used effectively with youngsters with varying abilities and from diverse ethnic and socio-economic backgrounds. The programs are also free of specific linguistic criteria and may be employed with non-English speaking children.

The learning process, structured by the teacher from the Open Framework, is usually paced by the child himself, with adaptation of the activities by the teacher to match the child's needs and interests. In well-run Open Framework classrooms teachers frequently report their surprise at the minimal discipline and management problems, which would seem to reflect the range of adaptations the framework allows.

In general, these curricula are organized to accomplish cognitive and language development based upon a theory of intellectual development. An open framework is provided for the teacher as a context within which she develops a specific program for the children in her classroom. Learning by the child is the product of his active involvement with the environment structured by the teacher. Examples of programs using this approach are Susan Gray's curriculum for the Demonstration and Research Center for Early Education; Merle Karnes' Ameliorative Preschool program; Herbert Sprigle's

Learning to Learn program; and our own Cognitive curriculum.

Child-centered. In this quadrant, representing *child initiates–teacher responds*, are the bulk of the traditional preschool programs as found on college campuses and in national projects such as Head Start. These curricula tend to focus on the development of the whole child, with emphasis on social and emotional growth. They are characterized by open and free environments with a generally permissive relationship between the teacher and the children and among the children themselves. Content revolves around things of interest or helpful to the child, such as community helpers, seasons, and holidays. There is a firm commitment to the idea that "play is the child's work" and recognition of the importance of the child's active involvement in his environment. Considerable attention is given to social adjustment and emotional growth through fantasy play, imitation of adult roles, rehearsal of peer relationships, and the careful development of the ability of the child to be independent of direct adult assistance.

If theory is involved in one of these programs, it is usually a theory of emotional development. The actual curriculum developed by the teacher comes mainly from her own intuitive understanding of child development on the one hand and her observation of the needs of her children on the other. In general, the hallmark of the Child-centered curricula is an open classroom with children free to express their individual interests and help create their own environment, and with a careful response by an experienced and intuitive teacher who has developed a sense of how to support this creative environment.

The major advantage of the Child-centered curricula is the complete openness to the needs of individual children. The program may be in direct harmony with the goals of both the parents and the professionals, reflecting the specific concerns of all involved. In addition, Child-centered curricula are highly reflective of the values given considerable prominence in society as a whole: independence, creativity, self-discipline, constructive peer relationships, etc. Also, since this is the dominant preschool program style, there is a vast reservoir of trained talent throughout the country, in colleges and universities, in organized national associations, and in the large number of programs currently utilizing these methods. In general, these curricula attempt to assist the child in his overall development through careful attention to his individual needs. The teacher draws upon her knowledge of child development to create a supportive classroom where learning is the result of the child's interaction with the materials, his classmates, and his teacher. While there may be agreement on general goals in most Child-centered programs, each teacher is responsible for the design of almost everything in her work. Typical of programs using this approach are the traditional nursery schools, the Bank Street College programs, Ron Henderson's Tucson Early Education Model, Glen Nimnicht's Responsive program, Robert Spaulding's Durham Education Improvement project, and, in spite of the odd "fit," the Montessori programs.

Custodial. In this quadrant, representing *teacher responds-child responds*, are programs which are of minimal value to children. At best these programs protect the child from physical harm and may be some improvement over extraordinarily bad social conditions. However, with the knowledge and resources available today, there is little excuse for maintaining custodial centers where teachers and children respond to nothing but physical needs since nothing is initiated.

Programmed, Open Framework, and Child-centered approaches differ widely on a number of important theoretical and practical issues, including curriculum supervision for staff, adaptability of the program to specific educational needs of minority and regional groups, breadth of curriculum focus, recommended procedures for child management, acceptability of the curriculum to teachers, and assumptions about how children learn. The basic question is, however, how does the particular curriculum model affect the immediate and long-term intellectual and academic performance of participating children? While there is considerable debate over the criteria to be employed, it is generally accepted that third-grade achievement scores on standardized tests are appropriate. There is less agreement about the use of intelligence tests, such as the Stanford–Binet, as a measure of immediate outcome at the end of the preschool experience. At the present time, however, no acceptable alternative measures are available for reliably measuring intellectual development or the more general capacities, from problem-solving ability to creativity. The scores from Piaget-based measures of cognitive abilities tend to be so closely correlated with Stanford–Binet scores as to make their use questionable as a substitute assessment procedure, though they may be invaluable in the design of research projects using Open Framework curricula. In any case, there is little basic information about the relative effectiveness of particular preschool curricula.

A few years ago, a review of preschool research found that the few programs which were effective in obtaining immediate gains on intellectual measures and some indication of later academic success could be classified as *Structured* (a category covering for the most part the Programmed and Open Framework curricula). "The conclusion is that preschool projects with the disadvantaged child must provide planned teacher action according to a specific developmental theory in which the primary goals are cognitive and language development . . . . The traditional nursery school methods [a category covering Child-centered] . . . are ineffective in accomplishing the basic goals of preschool intervention with the disadvantaged child" (Weikart 1967). A more recent review of several studies of Programmed, Open Framework, and Child-centered curricula reached the same conclusion: "Preschool programs . . . that provide highly structured experiences for disadvantaged children are more effective in producing cognitive gains than programs lacking these characteristics" (Bissell 1970). While such reviews underscore the ineffectiveness of Child-centered curricula with disadvantaged children, there is still the question whether Programmed or Open Framework models are more effective.

In an effort to answer this question, the Ypsilanti Preschool Curriculum Demonstration Project was established in the fall of 1967. The programs selected were a Cognitively Oriented curriculum (an Open Framework model) and a Language Training curriculum (a Programmed model). The *Cognitively Oriented curriculum* had been developed over the five years of the Ypsilanti Perry Preschool Project (Weikart 1967, 1970). This is a carefully structured program based on methods of "verbal bombardment" of our own design, principles of sociodramatic play as defined by Sara Smilansky, and principles derived from Piaget's theory of intellectual development. The *Language Training curriculum* was developed by Bereiter and Engelmann (1966) at the University of Illinois. This is a task-oriented program employing techniques from foreign language training; it includes the direct teaching of language, arithmetic, and reading. In order to complete the spectrum, a third program was established that would represent the traditional approach. This program, the *Unit-based curriculum* (a Child-centered model), emphasized the social-emotional goals and teaching methods of the traditional nursery school.

Children in the curriculum study were functionally retarded three- and four-year-olds from disadvantaged families living in the Ypsilanti school district. They were stratified according to sex and race and randomly assigned to one of the three treatment groups. Two teachers were assigned to each curriculum model, after they had an opportunity to express a preference. They taught class for half a day and then conducted a teaching session in the home of each of their children for ninety minutes every other week. The home teaching was executed in the same curriculum style as the classroom program in which the child was involved. Essential to the demonstration aspect of the project was that all three programs had clearly defined weekly goals. The curriculum implementation followed a carefully planned daily program designed independently by the three teams of teachers to achieve the goals of their own curricula. The provision for teacher involvement was a crucial aspect of the overall project.

Much to our surprise, each of the three programs did unusually well on all criteria (Weikart 1970), greatly exceeding improvement expected from general habituation and rapport leading to better test-taking ability. More importantly, the initial findings indicated no significant differences among the three curricula on almost all of the many measures employed in program assessment: several intelligence tests (average Stanford–Binet IQ gains in the three programs by three-year-olds of 27.5, 28.0, and 30.2 points in the first year); classroom observations; observations in free play settings; ratings of children by teachers and independent examiners; and evaluations by outside critics. These data were essentially replicated at the end of the project's second year. The basic conclusion is that the operational conditions of an experimental project are far more potent in influencing the outcome than the particular curriculum employed. The curriculum is more important for the demands it places upon the project staff in terms of operation than for what it gives the child in terms of content. Specifically, I would make two points regarding curriculum and the education of disadvantaged children.

1. *Broad curricula are equivalent.* As far as various preschool curricula are concerned, children profit intellectually and socio-emotionally from any curriculum that is based on a wide range of experiences. In almost the sense that Chomsky (1966) uses in talking about the development of linguistic competence, a child has the potential to develop cognitive skills and good educational habits if he is presented with a situation which requires their expression. Kohlberg (1968) concludes that a child needs broad general forms of active experience for adequate development of his cognitive abilities; a variety of specific types of stimulation are more or less functionally equivalent for development. In short, no specific curriculum has the corner on effective stimuli, and children are powerful enough consumers to avail themselves of what the market offers.

2. *The curriculum is for the teacher, not the child.* The primary role of curriculum is (1) to focus the energy of the teacher on a systematic effort to help the individual child to learn; (2) to provide a rational and integrated base for deciding which activities to include and which to omit; and (3) to provide criteria for others to judge program effectiveness,

so that the teacher may be adequately supervised. The successful curriculum is one that permits this structuring of the *teacher* to guide her in the task of adapting the theory she is applying to the actual behavior of the children. An unsuccessful curriculum is one that permits the teacher to give her energies to areas unrelated to her interaction with the child within the theoretical framework or fails to give her clear guidelines for using her time in planning, in interaction with the children, and in availing herself of critical supervision.

The basic implication of the findings of the Curriculum Demonstration Project, after two years, is that a shift in focus is necessary for preschool education. The heavy emphasis on curriculum development, while important, has greatly overshadowed the need for careful attention to the other components of program operation. Apparently when these components, including what we call the "staff model," are held as constant as possible, immediate results are not affected by the curriculum model.

But I have problems with my conclusions at this point, because by the third year of the study, while there were no significant differences on most general measures, the unit-based program was dropping out of the race gradually but surely, especially on a highly sensitive cognitive measure—the Stanford–Binet.

Table II–3 (pp. 62–63) presents the findings from the project on a year-of-operation basis. The waves of children entered as three-year-olds and attended the preschool for two years. The classes were organized across ages; that is, Wave 5 as four-year-olds and Wave 6 as three-year-olds attended school together, and the next year Wave 6 as four-year-olds and Wave 7 as three-year-olds attended school together. There was no dropout from any of the groups.

By the second replication in the third year of the project the unit-based program was not matching the outstanding record it had established during the first year, especially with the three-year-olds. At this point, given the purpose of the study—to compare three basic curriculum models—and given the general findings in the field, I could conclude that this

Child-centered curriculum didn't have the necessary power to make a significant impact on important dependent variables. Further, the use of a Child-centered curriculum with disadvantaged children could, as in other studies of this nature, be seriously questioned. However, the outstanding performance of the unit-based program the first-year, achieving parity with the other curricula at the three year-old level, and the fact that the drop occurred gradually rather than precipitately suggests problems other than simple statistical variation. It has therefore seemed important that the issues be explored more thoroughly.

When we took a closer look we found that while there are some inherent difficulties in the Child-centered model, the fault rested with me as project director. The issue rests in the "staff model," for differences in curriculum results occurred only when operational problems were left unresolved. To illustrate this key point I would like to present a description of the way the teachers in the three programs worked over the three years of the project; this was prepared by the supervising teacher, with whom I have worked for the last nine years, Mrs. Donna McClelland. Then I would like to present the statements prepared by the two teachers in the unit-based program. These descriptions were written at my request, three months after the termination of the project, with the instructions "to think back to how you felt about the years in the project and to note each year in succession."

The teachers have been assigned letters, which may be found in Table II–3, indicating the years they taught. The unit-based teachers taught together for the entire three years of the project.

Cognitive Curriculum: First Year, 1967–1968. Mrs. A and Mrs. B seemed to look forward to teaching, but at the same time they seemed apprehensive and insecure about it. They knew the project had a heavy investment in the curriculum and that the program had a theoretical framework. They wanted training. However, the training they received was very limited. We gave them books to read, written materials from the Perry Project, and some ideas about setting up the classroom. Because of *our* limited knowledge, we gave them only about half of the curriculum framework—the cognitive goal areas. Mrs. B was a brand new teacher, confident, with a lot of warmth and concern for children, extremely intelligent, and able to pick up the idea of the curriculum quickly. Mrs. A was an experienced teacher; she cared about the children. She was a good teacher in another setting who wanted to learn the framework. She tried, but she just couldn't immerse herself in it as Mrs. B did. I think she failed because we didn't know how to help her.

Both teachers worked very hard, and they were almost too rigid about their plans. They discussed the children, planned together, and shared ideas. It was a shared leadership. Mrs. A, with her years of experience, contributed many ideas for activities, and Mrs. B was secure enough to be able to use the ideas within the proper context. Even though she respected Mrs. A as an older, more experienced person, Mrs. B was forceful enough to speak up when she felt she was right. The curriculum made sense to Mrs. B very early. She committed herself to reading and learning more about it and demanded supervision from me.

Cognitive Curriculum: Second Year, 1968–1969. The beginning of the second year brought a new teacher to the classroom, Mrs. C. She was a beginning teacher, had little confidence in her own ability, and she leaned heavily on Mrs. B. She was eager, enthusiastic, and excited about the curriculum; she loved the children, devoted a great deal of time to planning and discussing them with the other teacher, and spent much extra time preparing materials. At mid-year, when Mrs. B left the classroom to become a project consultant, Mrs. C was capable of taking on the leadership of the teaching team. Although she understood what she was doing, she would not assume the leader role. Mrs. D, the new teacher, supposedly had some background in Piagetian theory, but she turned out to be strongly entrenched in the traditional approach. She wanted the children to learn by themselves once she provided the materials, and she wanted them to be creative above all. She didn't see that the cognitive curriculum started from the bottom to make it possible for children to operate that way. Mrs. C was very much influenced by Mrs. D, and they were off on all kinds of side roads with nothing much accomplished the rest of the year. Mrs. D was strong-willed and did things her way, which meant she had a great deal of trouble accepting the authority of the supervision provided. Mrs. D also seemed threatened by the children, not knowing how to manage them when she was confronted with a group teaching situation where she was responsible for directing the activity and holding the attention of the children. She preferred the freer work-time situations where the quality of her interaction could be different.

The teachers planned together well, talked everything over, wrote everything together. There was so much togetherness it was inefficient.

Cognitive Curriculum: Third Year, 1969–1970. The third year started about where the second year left off. The teachers were the same, with one major difference. They knew they had to operate the cognitive program in a particular way after a confrontation with the director at the end of the second year. They were subdued, but they seemed to want to successfully operate the program. It was necessary to be very direct with them at times to keep them on the track and to encourage Mrs. C to assert herself and not let Mrs. D dominate her.

As the year progressed Mrs. D learned to manage the children and not blame all unpleasant behavior on a child's emotional state. She learned to work on the level of the children. She began to understand the cognitive framework. When she didn't seem to understand, she tried hard to accept the authority of the supervisor. Mrs. C began to speak up when she had an opinion and even sided with the supervisor occasionally.

Whatever time and energy that were left went to improving implementation of the curriculum.

Language Training Curriculum: First Year, 1967–1968. Both Mrs. E and Mrs. F seemed eager to try the Language Training program. Each had a strong interest in teaching language and enthusiastically approached the task of outlining what they would teach from the Bereiter and Engelmann (1966) book, *Teaching Disadvantaged Children in the Preschool.* It was a tremendous task; the book was all they had from which to start planning. Mrs. E outlined and taught language, and Mrs. F outlined and taught reading. Arithmetic was shared. The teacher-aide was assigned the semistructured time which included work-sheets from the language, reading, and arithmetic lessons, reading stories, and juice time. The initial plan was to switch the teaching areas at mid-year so that both teachers could have a turn teaching language. They gave up the idea because planning was so time-consuming. That decision seemed to set the tone for the whole year: They worked hard and diligently but separately. While they spent hours planning, they seldom planned together or talked together about the children, even for the purpose of home visits. Both were extremely involved with the content that they were teaching, but somewhat detached from the children. They tried to follow the book exactly and viewed the group lessons and music as the important teaching times. The rest of the time the children were in school was left up to the aide. As a result, transitions, juice, and semistructured time were apt to be chaotic until the aide learned to manage the children. If the teachers finished teaching ahead of schedule they sent the children home early.

Both teachers had difficulty at first managing the children during group teaching. The children were so young and the tasks required sitting quietly and attending while the teacher talked or wrote on the blackboard.

Mrs. F was competent, self-assured, cool, and aloof, solving her own problems and rarely asking for help. She always wrote plans or worked on a home visit report whenever the staff met together. She seemed to relate to the children and the mothers the same way. She did what was expected of her and did it extraordinarily well, but seldom allowed herself to become personally involved.

Mrs. E was warmer and more involved with the children and the mothers. For example, she initiated and did most of the planning for the Christmas party for the children and their mothers. She became very excited about the language lessons. She had lots of ideas and spent extra time thinking of new and better ways to present the materials. She always seemed eager to talk to me about what she was doing, and she was always very open and receptive.

Language Training Curriculum: Second Year, 1968–1969. The second year began with two new teachers. Again, both teachers were interested in language development and eager to try the Language Training approach. Much of the organizational work had been done the year before. The lessons were outlined, and new materials from Illinois had been incorporated. Mrs. H had spent two or three days the spring before in the classroom with Mrs. E learning the program. Mrs. G came with some classroom experience and knew how to structure the day for the children so that the whole day was a learning experience. The teachers liked each other and enjoyed working together. Though one teacher taught reading and the other language, they discussed the progress of the children in each of their groups and planned together. They added two additional activities to their schedule: a fifteen-minute playtime the first thing in the morning, allowing the children to use puzzles, small blocks, beads, and other small educational toys freely, and a planned whole-group semi-structured time. They added this time because they felt the children needed to learn to cut, paste, color, and to play some group games. They also added a regular story time at the end of the day—Language Training style, of course. These additions allowed them to be creative and to make the program more compatible with their personal styles. The director relaxed about these changes after a consultant from the Illinois group gave her approval. The aide still handled semistructured time, helped with juice, and was given an arithmetic group to teach. The aide and the teachers were very much involved with the children throughout the day.

The leadership was shared equally by the teachers. They were both lively and dynamic. They tried to make the room attractive for the children, using pictures centered around what they were teaching and displaying the children's art work. They both put a great deal of extra time and effort toward planning parent meetings and toward making school interesting and fun for the children.

At one point there was dissatisfaction with the research aspect of the project, as the teachers felt they were not given enough information about the research. They were open and verbal about their complaint and a meeting was arranged to discuss this, which seemed to solve the problem.

Language Training Curriculum: Third Year, 1969–1970. The Language program started the third year with one new teacher. The new teacher was a friend of the hold-over teacher; they liked each other and worked well together. The quality of planning and involvement with the children continued at a high level.

The new teacher had been working with junior-high-level children before coming to the preschool, and she found it necessary to change her teaching style. Because her work had been with children of the same background as the preschool children, she felt the goals of the Language Training program were very important. The earlier the children were reached, the better. She took on the task of learning the program wholeheartedly and was able to adapt to and teach from the "cookbook."

Unit-based Curriculum: First Year, 1967–1968. Mrs. J and Mrs. K seemed motivated to provide a good school experience for the children. Mrs. J seemed to have more of an idea how to go about setting up the program; she assumed the leadership and appeared to generate most of the enthusiasm. Mrs. K was very emotionally involved with personal problems which were almost more than she could cope with at the time, and for a while she seemed grateful for the structure Mrs. J provided. They talked together about the children and shared ideas when planning activities and working out classroom problems. As time went along Mrs. K assumed more responsibility for the classroom and seemed to assert herself more. They both spent time outside of school hours preparing materials for the classroom in order to provide the best possible experience for the children. They worked diligently on group meetings for the mothers, preparing displays of the children's work and providing fancy refreshments. They liked having a classroom to themselves, where they could organize the room and use the materials in the way they felt was appropriate for their program. They had close contact with me, which seemed to be very important to them. Both were there regularly, and neither was sick more than a day or two.

They allowed the children a lot of freedom and had two or three children who were obvious discipline problems. They solved this by providing more structure through the daily routine and limiting the materials in the environment. Both seemed to like the children and to enjoy working with them.

The transfer of the class to another schoolhouse in mid-year to provide additional space for their program was traumatic for them. First, they had to change class time from morning to afternoon, forcing a reorganization of their whole schedule. Second, their classroom had to be structured in a different way because they now shared the room with the cognitive program. Third, they no longer had the same amount of contact with me. As a result, they seemed to feel left out and alone. Fortunately the move came late in the year.

Unit-based Curriculum: Second Year, 1968–1969. The program began the second year on about the same plane that it ended the first year—with the teachers somewhat discouraged and disgruntled. They became more and more aware of the emphasis put on the cognitive program by the many visitors to the project. They did less formal planning and seemed to become less and less enthusiastic as time went on. Mrs. J seemed to reflect this feeling more than Mrs. K. Mrs. K seemed to get more satisfaction from her work with the children than Mrs. J. Mrs. J began having car trouble, coming late, and going home just a little earlier than usual, leaving Mrs. K to clean up and get the classroom ready for the children. Mrs. K began to resent Mrs. J's behavior, but she would not be open about it and discuss it with her. I tried to help by offering to discuss it with the two of them. Mrs. K became very upset and begged me not to do this. She seemed to feel it would make the situation worse. The addition of a special consultant just for their program did not help. Mrs. K took over more of the planning for her own activities in the classroom, and Mrs. J planned her own activities. There was little or no communication between the two. Mrs. J began a series of illnesses and was out of the classroom a good deal. I talked to Mrs. J about her responsibility to Mrs. K for sharing the planning and some of the classroom preparation, but it didn't help. During this period Mrs. B became a consultant and left the classroom. Mrs. J seemed to feel that she should have been considered for such a position and lost all interest in working with the children. The illnesses increased. In spite of all this, the classroom hung together and the children seemed to be happy and learning. Mrs. K showed more initiative, asserted herself more, but still refused to discuss her feelings with Mrs. J.

Unit-based Curriculum: Third Year, 1969–1970. The last year started where the second left off; attitudes were at a low level. Both teachers felt their program was a control program and that no one in the project really cared about it. Mrs. J continued to be sick more than was reasonable, and Mrs. K just planned from day to day. She continued to devote her time to the children when they were in the classroom. Mrs. J busied herself with "urgent" telephone calls to mothers and little "picking up" chores, almost anything to keep from interacting with the children. It was necessary to let Mrs. J know I was checking her absence forms to make sure all were counted and to speak to her about leaving early and coming late. We did allow the unit-based program to meet in the morning the third year, which at that point did not help much.

Toward the middle of the year, when the teachers began their writing for the curriculum booklets and the London conference was in view, things picked up some. More interest in planning together seemed to be generated, but it was spasmodic. It continued that way much of the rest of the year. Surprisingly, the classroom still looked quite attractive, with the kids happy and learning.

Unit-based Curriculum: First Year, 1967–1968, Mrs. K. Having never taught at the preschool level before, I found that I needed a great deal of help just learning how to handle the children. The classroom was too small, only adding to the general confusion. We changed the routine frequently, and eliminated many toys. Later in the year, we moved to another school where we were provided with more space.

I felt confused, anxious, bewildered, frustrated, and depressed, because I didn't feel that the children were really learning anything.

Unit-based Curriculum: Second Year, 1968–1969, Mrs. K. I started out this year with a great deal of enthusiasm, I tried new ideas, established limits, discipline problems eased, children were more responsive.

The program goals, however, were still fuzzy. We were advised to concentrate on socialization among children and to just play with them. We did!

The interruptions in the classroom from researchers and visitors were annoying. It was very difficult to concentrate on the children when there was so much confusion.

Unit-based Curriculum: Third Year, 1969–1970, Mrs. K. There was obviously very little enthusiasm for our program, but I still felt that it was basically a good program. I also felt we could offer more in educational growth. We were reluctant to try anything new because it might be too similar to goals in other programs.

We used the same techniques and ideas developed over the past two years. It seemed rather dull to me, but the children had always done well in the past. Besides I was tired of trying to push, push, push. At times I felt that I was the only one interested in the children's development. It was very difficult to talk about the children with Mrs. J because she simply wasn't interested. She almost seemed to avoid the classroom whenever she could. It really bothered me that she didn't interact with the children more. It was also discouraging that often we had neither a definite plan to follow nor definite goal areas in which to work.

Unit-based Curriculum: First Year, 1967–1968, Mrs. J. Year one of the project was probably the best from my point of view. Everything was so new and the whole idea sounded rather fascinating. Then, too, I couldn't help but be very enthusiastic because it seemed that I, as a teacher, was a vital link in the whole operation. The staff was small (or at least seemed so to me), and staff meetings and contacts were friendly and informal.

I think another reason why I look back on the first year as most enjoyable is that policies, etc., were not so hard and fast. Ideas were constantly being introduced, discussed, and decided upon. And, whether this was actually true or not, I felt a part of it. Also, I felt I was a part of a developing curriculum, since we were not given a book as in the language training curriculum, nor did we have a previously developed curriculum as in the cognitive program. Rather, we were more or less on our own to choose things we felt were important.

It's difficult to recall a lot of the feelings I had during that first year. One thing for sure, though, I remember that our main focus was the children and our first job was teaching. To this end we had adequate time for planning, evaluating, meeting with the supervisor, etc.

To sum up the first year is to have favorable thoughts. There were three programs in progress, yet I never felt any competition between them. Rather, I felt very strongly that what I was doing was helping the children, and the other programs were helping also, but we had different approaches. Thinking about how much the children gained or which program gained the most was irrelevant. I was doing what I felt was best within the loose traditional framework from which we operated.

Unit-based Curriculum: Second Year, 1968–1969, Mrs. J. Year two to me represents the year the organization grew. Everytime we had a meeting new faces seemed to ease out of the woodwork. To this day, I do not know what some of the new faces did or how they fitted into the overall picture. (I don't know how much of this staff was anticipated at the onset of the project. Knowing what the project goals were and just what the overall picture was like would have put many things in perspective.) The new faces meant more formal meetings and also what I felt was a real communication gap. I felt that at times the right hand didn't know what the left hand was doing, yet the right hand made the decisions for the left hand to follow.

Research played an increasingly important role this year. I knew from the onset of the project that it was research-oriented. I knew, of course, that my role in the project was not to be a researcher but a teacher. Yet it became difficult to effectively carry out this role at times. I felt this was very unfortunate, for I think that a more cooperative attitude should have been established; teachers and researchers should have been working together as a team. We were supposed to be a team since we were members of the same project, but at times it appeared that major divisions existed: the teachers felt that the children were most important, while the researchers placed inanimate data as uppermost.

Unit-based Curriculum: Third Year, 1969–1970, Mrs. J. The third year of the project was the most dissatisfying of the three. For one thing, it seemed as though there was an underlying current that this was the last year—this is the last year, so let's hurry up and get it over with. Perhaps I generated a lot of this feeling within myself, for many times I felt that I was fighting a losing battle. It seemed quite obvious that the unit-based curriculum was one step under the low man on the totem pole. Our weekly curriculum meetings with our supervisor vanished and it seemed we were left to do whatever we chose. Whatever we did was "OK," yet I had the feeling that everyone felt that this curriculum wouldn't make it anyway. I found many of these views most frustrating, for I felt that if this was going to be a valid research project, one program should not be favored over the others. Frustrations were very high at times, for I felt this situation was very obvious and accepted. So the unit-based curriculum went on its merry way.

Writing played a significant role during the third year, and I welcomed this. We really had an opportunity to discuss more things, place some priorities, and generally get a better understanding of what we were actually doing in the classroom. Although we constantly handed our materials in for the booklet, I thought that ultimately the vast majority of the writing would be placed in the file (under dead), which turned out not to be true.

Outside demands were high the last year. We were expected to complete materials for research as usual. Added to this was the filming and people coming into the classroom collecting various kinds of information. Here again, I felt a more co-operative attitude could have been established, making everyone's work more pleasant.

Of all the feelings that stand out in the third year, the most emphatic is the feeling of being "the forgotten program" and the feeling that there wasn't much concern about what we did. It's difficult to keep enthusiasm high when confronted with such thoughts. Nevertheless, I did do the best I could.

How Can We Guarantee Preschool Effectiveness?

While the data are not complete for the Curriculum Demonstration Project, and we must await the long-term follow-up study as the children progress through elementary school, I find myself at a very different place from that I had projected back in 1966 when the project was conceptualized. I had expected to find immediate differences on most measures among the three curriculum models. Instead I found that during the time I was able to maintain equal momentum and staff commitment for the three programs, we obtained equal results on most measures, from standardized intelligence tests to classroom observations and teacher ratings. When this momentum was lost in the unit-based program, as can be seen in the above reports, the data began to shift. Clearly, the results of the different programs directly reflect staff model, not curriculum model, effects. While the unit-based teachers and Mrs. McClelland indicate that the classes were proceeding happily enough to look good to observers, the heart of the operation was missing and the children were marking time. From this situation, two essential points emerge regarding the operation of effective preschools:

1. *Planning.* Detailed planning for daily operation is absolutely critical. Experienced teachers can "wing it" without

plans by following routine practices which both they and the children slide into without trouble. However, the moment planning as an organized force ceases or diminishes in its central focus, program quality drops. Planning brings the adults in the program together and forces an integration of their ideas, so that they respond with purpose to the children. It produces a forward momentum, a pacing to the program that creates novelty and excitement for the children as well as the staff. It serves as a clearinghouse for interpersonal feelings that make the difference in how the staff relate to one another and the children. It produces in teachers a clarity of perception of each child, especially when part of the process is evaluation of completed curriculum activities. It provides a forum where the ideas generated by the method or theory being followed can be expressed and discussed to give an overview and total direction. Basically, it is highly satisfying to outline the major problems children face in dealing with the world as represented by the classroom and plan ways of facilitating the resolution of these problems. However, planning is also one of the most difficult things to ask of a teaching staff.

From reading the evaluations of the supervisor it is apparent that the three programs planned differently. In the Programmed model, planning did not have a central role because the lessons had already been planned for the teachers by the program developers. Since each teacher had to plan for her own groups, and subject areas were divided between them, planning was done individually in this program. In the Open Framework and Child-centered models, team planning was a daily function of a teaching staff that worked in the classroom. This approach is obviously vulnerable to problems resulting from interpersonal conflict, the more so if, as in the unit-based program, there are problems with supervision.

2. *Supervision.* While planning integrates the basic content and expression of the program, supervision makes it happen. As problems developed in the unit-based program, supervision became more difficult and was gradually reduced. I, as project director, failed to recognize the importance of what was happening and to act forcefully to redirect the situation.

Adequate supervision forces the teachers to consider the central issues of their curriculum model. It helps the staff to recognize when they are getting off the track or marking time. The supervisor gives direct assistance to the classroom team by underscoring the real problems. She reviews the plans the teachers have prepared and observes their implementation in the classroom. The supervisor raises questions for the staff about program operation, planning, and general functioning. She is the referee for the many problems within the team, bringing difficulties into the open rather than allowing them to be smoothed over; since genuine problems with children and among staff are the basis for program improvement, to smooth them over is to avoid the opportunity for development they present. The supervisor provides in-service training based upon the knowledge she has gained from her classroom observations. This training can include demonstration teaching and videotaping of key lessons or activities. On the whole, the supervisor serves as the balance wheel in the operation of the curriculum model, maintaining through supportive services, dedication, and knowledge the momentum that the staff has generated. These functions were carried out to differing degrees in the several models. The Programmed curriculum needed the least amount of attention from the supervisor; little beyond the usual function of meeting with the teachers to insure adherence to the model. The teacher-proof scripted materials effectively limited the range of potential behaviors of the teachers and directed their energy. On the other hand, the Open Framework staff needed and received considerable attention to integrate the theoretical base of their program with the classroom activities. The Child-centered program proved difficult to supervise. The program was based on the general knowledge of child development of the two staff members, and they were encouraged to design their own program, emphasizing those things they thought important. This freedom of the teachers limited the supervisor's role to general advice. The global and imprecise nature of the unit-based curriculum may be one reason why it was so hard to supervise.

In order to operate an effective preschool, then, the conclusion suggested by the findings of the Curriculum Demonstration Project is that any project must have an effective staff model which provides at least two major elements: planning and supervision. This finding suggests a third dimension for the diagram presented in Figure II–1; that is, *staff model intensity*. It has been our experience that whether a curriculum is Programmed, Open Framework, Child-centered, or eclectic, there must be a high intensity of planning and supervision in one form or another to assure success. The unit-based curriculum was not entirely successful because the intensity of planning and supervision was not sustained.

CONCLUSIONS

What amazes me again and again as I read over the critiques of the three years of the Curriculum Demonstration Project and think back over the last eight years of preschool research is the naïveté and even egotism with which I and perhaps some of my fellow researchers tended to approach the problems of curriculum, teaching, and learning for disadvantaged children. We constantly talked about the things that "they" are going to have to do in order to learn. And "they" are both the children and the teachers. We proceeded to develop materials and sophisticated devices to help us ritualistically enact some of our pet theories. When these procedures didn't work it was always the child or the teacher who failed, never us and certainly never our model. Of course, there are better ways of doing things, better equipment, books, procedures; but better because they help us do the job more efficiently, not because they are new or different. However, these things are not central to the good that can happen when an adequately organized group of teachers tackles the problems of nurturing young children.

What the data from this Curriculum Demonstration Project do for me is force me to take a close look at my personal philosophy of education; that is, how I feel about my role in working with teachers and children, and how I feel about basic values such as creativity, academic skills, independent thought, cooperation, initiative, and responsibility. For these data say to me that I'm free to select or mix any curriculum model which is compatible with my basic educational goals and the goals of the group I serve. And I can make that program effective by employing an intense staff model. It's clear that I'm still talking about short-term results because the long-term data are not available. It's also clear that certain curricula are much more difficult to implement than others. But I do not have to wait for *the* curriculum; I am free to develop or employ any curriculum that I believe can be adapted to the needs of the children and the requirements of the staff model.

INTRODUCTION TO TABLES

There were five project replications between 1962 and 1966, with approximately twelve children per group entering each year. The declining group sizes in the tables reflect the fact that groups starting in the last replications had not yet reached the higher grade levels at the time of analysis.

The data were collected at the time children entered the preschool and every spring thereafter for most instruments. The following notation denotes collection times:

Preschool:	FEY	Fall entering year
	SEY	Spring entering year
	S2Y	Spring second year
Public School:	SKG	Spring kindergarten
	S1G	Spring first grade
	S2G	Spring second grade
	S3G	Spring third grade

Empty columns in the table indicate that data were not collected for a particular instrument at the time indicated by that column. Also, the first year's experimental and control groups contained some four-year-old children who received only one year of preschool, deflating the spring second-year group size somewhat. All other children entered at age three and had two years of preschool.

Table II–1. Stanford–Binet IQ Results—Experimental vs. Control
(Summary of Group Sizes, Group Means, and F-Ratios)

			Time of data collection				
	FEY	SEY	S2Y	SKG	S1G	S2G	S3G
Group size:							
Experimental	58	58	44	45	33	21	13
Control	65	65	49	52	37	24	15
Group IQ means:							
Experimental	79.7	95.8	94.7	90.5	91.2	88.8	89.6
Control	79.1	83.4	82.7	85.4	83.3	86.5	88.1
F-Ratio	<1	39.78	25.36	4.58	8.26	<1	<1
Significance	n.s.	<.01	<.01	<.05	<.01	n.s.	n.s.

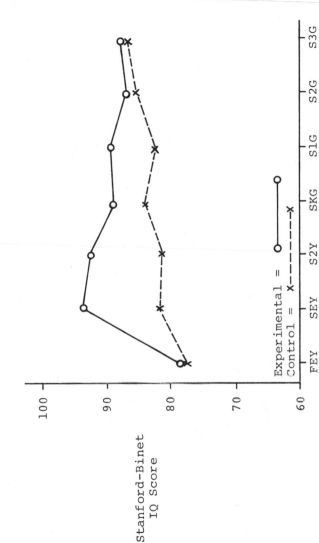

GRAPH OF STANFORD-BINET GROUP MEANS
Experimental vs. Control

Table II-2. California Achievement Test Total Battery Results—
Experimental vs. Control
(Summary of Group Sizes, Group Means, and F-Ratios)

				Time of data collection			
	FEY	SEY	S2Y	SKG	S1G	S2G	S3G
Group size:							
Experimental					33	20	13
Control					37	23	15
Group RAW score means:							
Experimental					90.7	146.0	199.9
Control					71.5	121.2	116.5
F-Ratio					4.27	2.92	11.61
Significance					<.05	n.s.	<.01

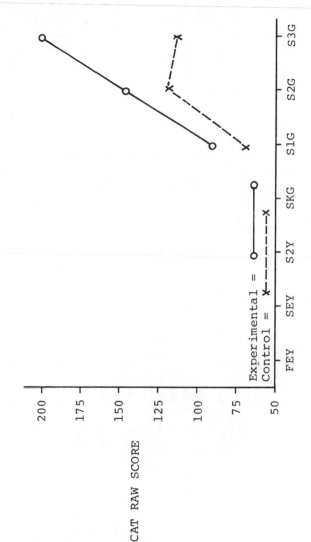

GRAPH OF CAT GROUP MEANS
Experimental vs. Control

Table II–3. Stanford–Binet Data for Three Years of Program Operation

	Fall entering year		Spring entering year				Spring second year		Difference between fall entering and spring second year
	Mean	Standard deviation	Mean	Standard deviation	Difference		Mean	Standard deviation	
1967–68									
Cognitive (N = 5) teachers A & B	83.2	4.8	110.8	12.3	+27.6	(N = 11)	98.6	12.81	+23.3[c]
Language (N = 8) teachers E & F	84.4	3.2	114.6	6.1	+30.2	(N = 8)	98.2	9.41	+24.3[d]
Unit-based (N = 8) teachers J & K	73.6	6.9	101.1	7.1	+27.5	(N = 8)	94.1	2.41	+17.7[e]
1968–69									
Cognitive (N = 7) teachers B/D & C	79.9	7.3	102.3	13.8	+22.4		101.2	10.4	+18.0
Language (N = 8) teachers G & H	78.3	6.0	102.3	13.9	+24.0		113.1	9.7	+28.7
Unit-based (N = 8) teachers J & K	84.3	3.6	101.9	7.4	+17.6		93.7	6.6	+20.1

Wave labels (1967–68): Wave 6; Wave 5b; Wave 6

Wave labels (1968–69): Wave 7; Wave 6; Wave 7

1969–70

Cognitive (N = 10) teachers C & D	80.3	6.9	97.1	10.8	+16.8	95.3	17.9	+15.4
Language (N = 9) teachers H & I	81.6	3.2	107.3	6.9	+25.7	100.4	9.6	+22.1
Unit-based (N = 9) teachers J & K	83.0	4.9	95.4	8.3	+12.4	90.5	9.2	+6.2

Wave 7

Wave 8[a]

[a] Wave 8 did not have home teaching.
[b] Wave 5 is the transition wave from the 1962–67 Perry Project.
[c] Fall entering year 75.3—attended two years of preschool as three- and four-year-olds.
[d] Fall entering year 73.9—tested only as three-year-olds, attended Language program as four-year-olds.
[e] Fall entering year 76.4—tested only as four-year-olds, fall 1967, attended Unit-based program as four-year-olds.

REFERENCES

Beller, E. K. 1969. The evaluation of effects of early educational intervention on intellectual and social development of lower-class, disadvantaged children. In E. Grothberg, (ed.), *Critical issues in research related to disadvantaged children*. Princeton: Educational Testing Service.

Bereiter, C., and Engelmann, S. 1966. *Teaching disadvantaged children in the preschool*. Englewood Cliffs, N.J.: Prentice–Hall.

Bissell, J. S. 1970. The cognitive effects of preschool programs for disadvantaged children. National Institute of Child Health and Human Development.

Brittain, C. 1966. Preschool programs for culturally deprived children. *Children*, July–August.

Chomsky, N. 1966. *Cartesian linguistics*. New York: Harper and Row.

Di Lorenzo, L. T., and Salter, R. 1968. An evaluative study of prekindergarten programs for educationally disadvantaged children. *Exceptional children* 35: 111–19.

Freeman, R. 1970. The alchemists in our public schools. In J. Hellmuth (ed.), *Disadvantaged child*, vol. 3, *Compensatory education: A national debate*. New York: Bruner–Mazel.

Fuller, E. 1960. *Values in early childhood education*. Washington, D.C.: National Educational Association.

Gray, S. 1969. Selected longitudinal studies of compensatory education—a look from the inside. Paper prepared for the annual meeting of the American Psychological Association.

Gray, S., and Klaus, R. A. 1965. An experimental preschool program for culturally deprived children. *Child Development*, 36: 887–898.

Hawkridge, D., Chalupsky, A., and Roberts, A. 1968. *A study of selected exemplary programs for the education of disadvantaged children*. Palo Alto: American Institutes for Research in the Behavioral Sciences.

Hodges, W. L., McCandless, B. R., and Spicker, H. H. 1967. *The development and evaluation of a diagnostically based curricu-*

lum for preschool psychosocially deprived children. United States Department of Health, Education, and Welfare.

Horowitz, F., and Paden, L. 1970. The effectiveness of environmental intervention programs. In B. Caldwell and H. Ricciuti (eds.), *Review of child development research.* Vol. 3. New York: Russell Sage Foundation.

Karnes, M. B., et al. 1969. *Investigations of classroom and at-home interventions. Research and development program on preschool disadvantaged children. Final Report.* Vol. I. University of Illinois, Urbana: Institute of Research for Exceptional Children, May 1969.

Kohlberg, L. 1968. Early education: A cognitive–developmental view. *Child Development* 39: 1013–62.

Kraft, I., Fuschillo, J., and Herzog, E. 1968. *Prelude to school: An evaluation of an inner-city program.* Washington, D.C.: U.S. Department of Health, Education, and Welfare. Children's Bureau.

Sears, P. S., and Dowley, E. M. 1963. Research on teaching in the nursery school. Pp. 811–64 in N. L. Gage (ed.), *Handbook of research on teaching.* Chicago: Rand McNally.

Skeels, H. M. 1966. Adult status of children with contrasting early life experiences: A follow-up study. *Monographs of the Society for Research in Child Development* 32:2.

Swift, J. 1964. Effects of early group experiences: the nursery school and day nursery. In M. Hoffman & L. Hoffman (eds.), *Review of child development research.* New York: Russell Sage Foundation.

Weikart, D. P. 1967. Preschool programs: Preliminary findings. *Journal of Special Education* 1: 163–81.

————. 1970. A comparative study of three preschool curricula. In J. Frost (ed.), *Disadvantaged child* (2nd ed.). New York: Houghton Mifflin.

Weikart, D. P., Deloria, D., Lawser, S., and Wiegerink, R. 1970. *Longitudinal results of the Ypsilanti Perry Preschool Project.* Ypsilanti, Michigan: High/Scope Educational Research Foundation.

Weikart, D. P., Rogers, L., Adcock, C., and McClelland, D. 1971. *The cognitively oriented curriculum: A framework for preschool teachers.* Washington, D.C.: National Association for the Education of Young Children.

Westinghouse Learning Corporation. 1969. *The impact of Head Start: An evaluation of the effects of Head Start experience on children's cognitive and effective development.* Preliminary draft of April 1969. Westinghouse Learning Corporation: Ohio University.

ORALIE MC AFEE
College of Education
University of Northern Colorado
Greeley, Colorado 80631

III · AN INTEGRATED APPROACH TO EARLY CHILDHOOD EDUCATION*

THE SPECIFIC GROUP which is the school's concern in Greeley, Colorado, is best described in terms of the families and children involved during the school year 1970–71.

The children were three-, four-, and five-year-olds, all prekindergarten. Twenty-five were of Spanish, Spanish-Indian, and Mexican background; two were black; and three were white.

The average grade level attained by the parents was below the seventh; five parents had never been to school at all. The average number of children in the family was between four and five, ranging from one to ten.

The children met at least three of the following criteria:

1. Economic conditions in the home were at or below Head Start economic guidelines.

* Only through the combined efforts of many individuals and community organizations can the implementation and research described in this project be carried out. The New Nursery School's programs for children, parents, and teachers have been supported by the Boettcher Foundation of Denver, the University of Northern Colorado, the Office of Economic Opportunity, and the United States Office of Education. Especially involved have been Dr. Edward J. Kelly and Dr. Beatrice Heimerl.

The research reported here was undertaken as part of Contracts No. 1260, B99–4743 and B00–5086 with the Office of Economic Opportunity, Executive Office of the President, Washington, D.C. 20506. The opinions expressed herein are those of the author and should not be construed as representing the opinions or policy of the United States government.

2. Educational level of the parents was at or below ninth grade.
3. The family was receiving assistance from public welfare or other agencies.
4. Older siblings had or were having school difficulty.
5. One or both parents were absent from the home.
6. Speech was different from that expected in school, as evidenced by lack of fluency, use of dialect, or primary language other than English used by parent or parent-substitute.

An attempt is made to maintain an age and sex balance of fifteen boys and fifteen girls, fifteen three-year-olds and fifteen four-year-olds. Children are grouped on a mixed age and sex basis and attend school three hours and fifteen minutes a day, five days a week.

Ideally, the children enter at age three, stay for two years, and then enter kindergarten in the Greeley schools. However, not all the children attended for two years; records have been kept on those children who attended for a year or more.

CURRICULUM CONSIDERATIONS

The rapid expansion of group care for young children, especially those from disadvantaged homes, has made the continued development, refinement, and evaluation of curricula for the prereading child essential. All-day, extended-day, and year-round programs require that careful consideration be given to the educational experiences offered in such programs and the methodology used.

The development and evaluation of such appropriate curricula and methodology for the disadvantaged child have been the goal of the New Nursery School. The school began, and has continued to evolve, as an experiment in developing an environment responsive to the child's interests and needs, quite aware of the school's obligation to help the child learn, yet convinced that how the child learns is at least as important as what he learns.

Drawing from the humanistic tradition as well as modern

research and theory, it has attempted to show that both content and process objectives suitable for early education can be achieved without drill, pressure, or a rigid curriculum. The cognitive elements in the program are not something set apart from or in addition to the classroom experiences, but are consciously interwoven into planned learning experiences, classroom routines, and children's spontaneous play.

The schematic chart, shown as Table III–1, presents the approach used and is a synthesis-analysis summary of the processes and products involved. The variables indicated in the schematic chart are then amplified or further described.

The capabilities desired of the children after completing the school experiences are defined under five primary objectives. (Examples are listed under each objective.)

1. Increasing sensory and perceptual acuity.
   a. The child is able to use all his senses as a means of finding out about his environment.
   b. The child begins to interpret accurately what his senses encounter.
2. Developing language ability.
   a. The child is able to label and describe objects, actions, events, and relationships in his environment.
   b. The child is able to use words to remember and predict events, to contrast and compare.
   c. The child is able to communicate in words and sentences which can be understood by others.
   d. The child is able to comprehend and express certain fundamental concepts which seem to expedite further learning (see below).
3. Developing conceptual ability.
   The child is able to comprehend and express concepts such as:
   —color
   —shape (including letters and numerals)
   —size (including relative size)
   —number
   —relative and contrasting location (in front of, behind, in, out)

Table III-1. Systems Approach to New Nursery School Project

Need

New Nursery School

Objectives

To develop children's

1. Sensory and perceptual acuity
2. Language ability
3. Conceptual ability
4. Problem solving ability
5. Positive self-concept

To provide for

6. Training preservice college students
7. Training inservice teachers and aides
8. Demonstration of appropriate and effective curricula and methods
9. Dissemination

Methods and Procedures

1. Suitable curricula
2. Open, responsive educational process
3. Comprehensive services
4. Parent organization and involvement—home visitation/mobile library; classroom experience, parent training workshops
5. Practicums, demonstrations, consultants, visitations, workshops
6. Written and filmed materials
7. Speeches

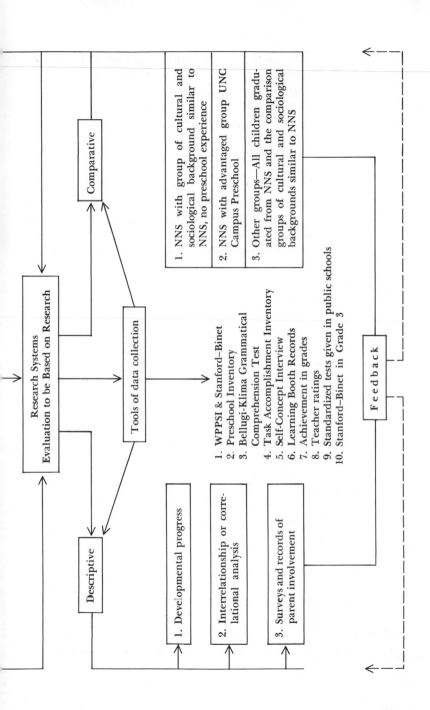

Research Systems
Evaluation to be Based on Research

Comparative

Descriptive

Tools of data collection

1. NNS with group of cultural and sociological background similar to NNS, no preschool experience

2. NNS with advantaged group UNC Campus Preschool

3. Other groups—All children graduated from NNS and the comparison groups of cultural and sociological backgrounds similar to NNS

1. WPPSI & Stanford–Binet
2. Preschool Inventory
3. Bellugi-Klima Grammatical Comprehension Test
4. Task Accomplishment Inventory
5. Self-Concept Interview
6. Learning Booth Records
7. Achievement in grades
8. Teacher ratings
9. Standardized tests given in public schools
10. Stanford–Binet in Grade 3

1. Developmental progress

2. Interrelationship or correlational analysis

3. Surveys and records of parent involvement

Feedback

71

—contrasting or opposing conditions (hot/cold, with/without, same/different, and/or)

—relative number (more/fewer)

—relative mass or volume (more/less)

—relative weight

4. Developing problem-solving ability.
   a. The child is able to work on his own to attempt to solve problems.
   b. The child is able to use certain processes of learning which enable him to solve problems, such as sorting and classifying, ordering, patterning, counting, making associations, eliminating known responses to arrive at an unknown, identifying which piece is missing out of a matrix or puzzle, and so forth.
5. Developing a positive self-concept.
   a. The child begins to develop an understanding of and pride in his cultural and ethnic heritage, and in his own community.
   b. The child is able to participate in classroom activities at his own pace and with his own style of operation, and to enjoy such participation.
   c. The child is able to respond to and say his first, last, and full name on request.
   d. The child is able to develop a positive relationship with adults and other children, as evidenced by seeking information and help, lack of fear, and other indicators of trust.

Although the program is a dynamic, changing one, certain principles concerning implementation guide its development:

1. The child is encouraged to choose the activities in which he wants to participate, and to set his own pace and style in working at them.
2. The child is actively, physically involved in the learning process.
3. The child is encouraged to experiment, explore, and make discoveries on his own.
4. The child participates in learning activities because he is interested and wants to learn, not because of external rewards or punishments.

Such careful delineation of objectives and methods is necessary to lend consistency, cohesiveness, and purpose. Without this, early education or, indeed, open education at any level is in danger of becoming merely a collection of unrelated activities. Unless the adults can set the goals and determine how they may be achieved, there is no standard by which to judge what is to be included in the program and why.

How are these methods implemented and the objectives attained? What does all this actually mean in operation? It means that a child is free to move from one activity to another in the classroom, staying a long time with one activity if he chooses, a short time with another activity, and probably not even participating in many activities on a given day. One child may become fascinated by sorting small rocks—painstakingly sorting and resorting until he has groupings with which he is satisfied. Another may come up with similar groupings in a fraction of the time by using a different method, then move on to something else. Still another may never touch the rocks but show with other materials that he has full command of the process.

It means that a child spends much time actively engaged with objects—putting together, taking apart, arranging, rearranging, ordering, fitting together, responding to words with physical actions, and having his actions responded to with words. He is not expected to learn through symbols or representations alone, although these means are very much a part of the process.

Much equipment and many materials are provided to encourage experimentation and exploration. Some of it is intended to help the children grasp a particular concept; some of it is "open-ended" so that closure is not expected. A typical example of the latter involves experimentation with what things sink and what things float. Children are given opportunities to predict, try out, verify or reject the prediction, and perhaps make guesses at "why." But no effort is made to fully explain to the child or to teach a rule which he might apply.

Perhaps more important than the materials and activities provided is the attitude of the adults. A child's attempts to solve problems on his own are valued, as are his often unexpected solutions and discoveries. Some instances of the sort of thing that happens follow.

A child working with geometric shapes at a magnetic board put two right isosceles triangles together to make a square, then arranged four to make a larger square, and arranged other squares to make an even larger square. All were then carefully ordered according to size.

A child arranging carpet samples in a pattern on the floor suddenly discovered and began showing the other children that when they rubbed their hands hard against the carpet their hands got hot, hot enough in fact to smell like smoke.

A child who was in the process of learning about rectangles helped put the unit blocks away. She held up in turn the unit, double unit, and quadruple unit and asked about each, "This is a rectangle?"

Such an attitude extends to language as well, where a narrow focus on *the* right way is avoided, unless it is very clear that only one answer applies. Even then, the imaginative response is valued. In the course of an episode involving gelatin dessert with fruit on the bottom, which was being turned "upside down" as it was served to help the children grasp this idea, one youngster objected, "No, I want mine up-side-up."

Teachers are very much involved in interaction with the children—interpreting, posing problems, guiding, teaching, and planning to assure that the experiences add up to something worth while. For within this context certain specific content should be learned by the children if objectives are to be achieved. And observation indicates that the learning of specific content enhances the child's ability to display such insights as those listed above.

Helping children learn size and position relationships, counting, simple classification, shapes, and other fairly specific ideas is relatively easy. So also is development of ways to teach certain less common curriculum items.

As an example, suppose a diagnostic test showed that the children didn't do well on comprehending the negative prefix "un"—untied, unloaded, and so forth. An advantaged group did enough better that probably some serious thought should be given to helping the experimental group grasp the significance of that commonly used form of negation or opposition. The next step is to run a check on the test. Perhaps the children actually use the construction even though they did not respond correctly on the test. The check indicates that they do seem to know *zip, button, tie,* and other such words, but use the same words for the undoing of the action, or simply "do dis."

So the task is clear: Help them to learn. How do young children learn? From many meaningful and specific situations and experiences. Having provided such a specific instance, a "happening" if you will, the teacher has the opportunity to respond to the young child with appropriate language—establishing thereby a calculated depth for the experience.

"Now that your truck is loaded, where are you going to unload it?"

"Fold the paper; now unfold the paper." (in spot painting)

"Unfold your napkin and put it in your lap."

"I'll help you untie the string on your jacket." (or unzip, unbutton, or unsnap)

Gradually this becomes:

"Do you want your cracker buttered or unbuttered?"

"Do you want cooked carrots or uncooked carrots?"

"Do you want lined or unlined paper?"

Then later:

"What's wrong with your shoestring?"

"What kind of carrots do we have today?" or

"What do you want me to do?" as a child points to a hard knot in the string of his hood or a stuck zipper.

We have helped the child acquire the idea and learn the words in carefully planned learning situations, in spontaneous play, and in routines. Now we expect him to use them in all these situations. It should be emphasized that not all the conceptual and language items the children need to know are this easy to develop.

At the time the school was begun, there was a definite need in the early education of children from low income families for approaches and curricula flexible and open enough to allow for individual and group variation and for incorporation of new insights and understandings; practical and economical enough to be duplicated by other programs with available resources; specific enough to be implemented by reasonably skilled teachers and assistants; and comprehensive enough to be a "whole," to contribute to the child's physical, emotional, social, and intellectual development, but with particular emphasis on intellectual development.

The development, demonstration, and evaluation of such a program continues to be the goal of the school. Selected evaluations of this approach to early childhood education will now be considered.

EVALUATION

Attempting to assess fairly the impact of a specific program on the human organism is difficult at best. This difficulty is compounded when the human organism in question is young, and the assessment is of aspects of human behavior whose mysteries continue to interest, intrigue—and defy—the philosopher, psychologist, and educator. In addition, one should always remember that there are other aspects of human behavior equally important which do not lend themselves to quantitative analysis. Attempts to evaluate that elusive characteristic called intelligence or the acquisition of specific content are concerned with only a portion of a total program—an important portion, yes, but not the totality.

Evaluation is, of course, subject to limitations of small sample size, missing data, age characteristics of the children, language difficulties, refusal of some children to be tested, affective reactions to testing, tester variability, mobility of experimental and comparison groups, and far from perfect matching of these groups. These are the conditions that prevail in most nonlaboratory development and evaluation projects. They reflect the difficulties encountered by early childhood centers in developing programs and evaluating their effectiveness, and particularly by centers concerned with children from low income families.

Despite these limitations, I have prepared a detailed statistical analysis of data involving several variables and groups shown in Table III–1. Twelve of the fourteen tables reporting those analyses will not be presented here, but they are available from me without charge. Instead, a brief summary of the results appears below.

Nine first-year pupils gained considerably (and statistically significantly) in personal-social responsiveness, associative vocabulary, numerical concept activation, and sensory concept activation from September 1969 to May 1970, as measured by the Caldwell and Soule (1967) Preschool Inventory. The New Nursery School program emphasizes specific content similar to much of that found in this inventory, so such a finding might well be expected. Also, of course, some of the gain over time is probably due to maturation of the child's nervous system, thereby enabling him to profit more from experiences in the preschool and elsewhere. This aspect is assessed to some extent later in the paper by means of a control group.

Results were similar for thirteen second-year pupils, but the gains from the beginning to the end of the year were not as great.

Fourteen second-year pupils scored considerably higher (eleven IQ points) on the verbal scale of the Wechsler Preschool and Primary Scale in the fall of 1970 than did fifteen comparison pupils, but they scored only three IQ points higher on the performance scale.

On eight out of nine color, counting, shape, relative size, and relative location tests (McAfee et al. 1969), first-year pupils (N = 10–13) improved greatly from September 1969 to May 1970. Only on comprehension of relative location was the gain small.

These inventories were also administered to an advantaged (Home Economics Preschool) group of children. They proved superior to the New Nursery School first-year children in all nine areas, but less so at the end of the school year than at its beginning.

Similar results with the same Task Accomplishment Inventory were obtained for the second year (i.e., four-year-old) pupils. It was apparent, however, that the second-year New Nursery School pupils did not gain at the rate the first-year pupils did. Although there are complicating factors, it is difficult to avoid the conclusion that the experiences offered the second-year pupils simply were not challenging enough. If, for example, a child can accurately count eight objects in September, there does not seem, logically, to be any reason why he cannot go well beyond that by May. Changes in emphasis have in fact been made to help the second-year children progress in a manner commensurate with their ability.

Another instrument administered was the Bellugi-Klima Test of Grammatical Comprehension (Bellugi-Klima 1968). It consisted of sixteen subtests evaluating such items as prepositions, conjunctions, the simple plural, position of noun and object in active and passive voice, and comparatives. Objects were placed in front of the child; he manipulated them in response to directions from the tester.

The New Nursery School and the Home Economics Preschool pupils took this test in November 1969 and May 1970. Both first-year and second-year New Nursery School groups (N's of fourteen each) made significant gains on the total score. However, the advantaged group began at the beginning of the first year where the New Nursery School pupils were at the end of the second year and made a substantial gain the first year. The New Nursery School children made particular progress on those items where curriculum emphasis was strong and curriculum development well under way, such as knowing the meaning of *more, less,* and *fewer,* the difference between *and* and *or,* and placement of the adjective modifier.

Examination of the results obtained on the two unstandardized instruments mentioned above suggests that the language and conceptual items evaluated are ones which tend to differentiate the child of a high income, high educational level background sharply from the child who has a low income, low educational level background. Also suggested is that a carefully planned program can help lessen those differences.

The identification of specific content, processes, and skills, which seem to contribute to school success and the lack of which seems to inhibit that success should afford a better curriculum guide than does the overly general description often employed. Language development and concept formation are goals of most early childhood programs, especially those concerned with children from areas of poverty. But *what* elements of language and *which* concepts? This study suggested that a more precise identification can be made and that differences in performance on those elements thus identified can begin to be lessened. The Bellugi-Klima Test of Grammatical Comprehension, in particular, indicated that the language differences found in many children from low income, low educational level homes are far deeper than vocabulary alone. They extend to structural and grammatical meanings as well. Methods and materials to lessen these differences have only begun to be constructed.

LONGITUDINAL STUDY

At the time of the 1970 analysis, five groups of children had gone on to public school from the New Nursery School. Not all these children had attended for two years. Records were kept on all children remaining in the Greeley area who attended the New Nursery School for one year or more. When each group entered kindergarten, a comparison group was selected as close in cultural and sociological background as could be found but without nursery school experience. In an effort to avoid children who had attended Head Start, children were sometimes selected who were more advantaged than the experimental group, especially since extensive efforts were made to recruit for the New Nursery School those children most in need of educational help before they started school. It is now necessary to go to small towns and rural areas close to Greeley to find children comparable, but with no Head Start or nursery school experience.

Data available from the public schools on these groups vary from year to year and school to school. One figure consistently available is attendance; the 1969–70 findings indicate that four of the five graduate groups have attendance records superior to their comparison groups. Comparable attendance records have been found in previous years. Regular attendance may well contribute to success in school. Because such regularity is not stressed among the particular group which is the primary concern of the New Nursery School, it may be indicative of attitude changes on the part of family and child. There is always the possibility that better attendance may be simply a function of selectivity of the experimental group— that children whose families consented to be involved in the first place and who kept their children in for a year or more had already achieved attitude changes. However, the extensive efforts made to recruit and keep the young children in school are not in keeping with that explanation. Those children who dropped out usually did so because they moved.

Three of the groups, the 1964–65, 1965–66, and 1966–67, took the Metropolitan Achievement Test in public school. Two of the New Nursery School groups scored higher than their comparison groups.

At the end of each school year teachers in the elementary schools were asked to give their opinion of each child's standing within his class in reading, arithmetic, independence, attention span, and appropriate behavior. In all cases the differences between the two groups were very slight, although three of the New Nursery School groups received rankings higher than their comparison groups.

Several direct measures of self-concept have been tried, none of which were satisfactory with the young children involved. An indirect measure, Stanley Coopersmith's Behavior Rating Form (Coopersmith 1967), is currently being used. Each spring teachers in the elementary schools are asked to rate children in the experimental and similar sample comparison groups on a ten-item, five-point scale describing behaviors presumed to be related to the child's self-esteem. According to Coopersmith (1967, p. 267), items "referred to such behaviors as the child's reaction to failure, self-confidence in a new situation, sociability with peers, and the need for encouragement and reassurance. . . . On theoretical and empirical grounds, the behaviors were assumed to be an external manifestation of the person's prevailing self appraisal." Four out of five of the New Nursery School groups had mean scores higher than their comparison groups, although in only one group was the difference statistically significant. The comparison group which excelled the experimental group did so by less than one point.

In January 1970 the Stanford–Binet Scale of Intelligence was administered to the 1965–66 New Nursery School graduates and the similar comparison group, at that time in third grade. Even though the children included in the experimental and comparison groups were from families considered Greeley residents, the number of children in the experimental group had dropped from twenty-one (21) to sixteen (16); the number in the comparison group fell from twenty-eight (28) to eleven (11) because the families had moved away from the area. The Stanford–Binet IQ mean for each group was raised when only the smaller number of children was considered, indicating that those children who moved were those who had made lower scores on this measure in fall 1966. Results for the Stanford–Binet test are shown in Table III–2.

Of course, the comparisons in Table III–2 depend on the assumption that, before the New Nursery School experience, the experimental subjects were not already considerably su-

Table III–2. Comparison of the Mean IQ Scores and Standard Deviations on the Stanford–Binet for the 1965–66 New Nursery School Graduates and the Similar–Sample Comparison Group

| Stanford–Binet administered in | New Nursery School 1965–66 graduates | | Similar Sample | | Mean differ- ence |
	Mean (S.D.)		Mean (S.D.)		
September 1966	N = 21	93.76 (12.18)	N = 28	83.75 (18.66)	10.01
September 1966	N = 16*	98.64 (10.18)	N – 11*	91.00 (15.33)	7.64
January 1970	N = 16*	98.31 (10.14)	N = 11*	91.90 (13.12)	6.41

* Children still available for testing in 1970.

perior to the control subjects in actual or potential Stanford–Binet ability. As explained above, great effort was made to avoid this direction of bias.

Results from the Metropolitan Achievement Test, on which the New Nursery School group did better than the comparison group, corroborate the results of the Stanford–Binet test. If such gains were made as a result of a preschool group experience, they have not been "washed out." The experimental group has maintained an advantage over the similar comparison group in school achievement tests, evident especially in mathematics but also in reading.

The class standing variables for these groups, obtained from ten teachers at six schools, show a difference in favor of the experimental group so slight as to be almost nonexistent. It is difficult to avoid the conclusion that existing differences in ability and achievement are overlooked in the classroom.

The intercorrelations of these three evaluations are shown in Table III–3. If the Stanford–Binet is supposed to be a good predictor of success in school, evidently there are other forces negating its prediction in these cases. Teacher ratings of children's class standing correlated rather poorly (.33 to .46) with the Stanford–Binet IQ scores, especially in reading. Class standings in the two academic areas of reading and arithmetic correlated rather well (.71) with scores on the standardized achievement test.

DISCUSSION

Discussion should perhaps be limited to research and its implications. However, sometimes research results take on added significance when placed in the larger context of current social and educational concerns.

It is ironic that concurrent with a trend toward the "opening up" of all of education in much the same way that preschools have always been, there is a trend toward "tightening down" in early childhood, toward making nursery schools and kindergartens more like the elementary grades. Yet there is

Table III–3. *Correlations among the Stanford–Binet IQ Scores, Class Standing Variables, and Metropolitan Achievement Test Scores*

| | Class standing variables | | | | | | Metropolitan achievement | |
	Reading	Arith-metic	Indepen-dence	Atten-tion	Behavior	Total	Reading	Mathe-matics
Stanford–Binet								
IQ	.33	.42	.36	.39	.46*	.36	.65*	.63*
Class standing variables								
Reading		.91*	.84*	.88*	.59*	.90*	.71*	.63*
Arithmetic			.87*	.89*	.62*	.89*	.72*	.71*
Independence				.95*	.77*	.98*	.72*	.83*
Attention					.79*	.96*	.85*	.85*
Behavior						.79*	.74*	.71*
TOTAL							.80*	.80*
Metropolitan achievement								
Reading								.90*

Note: Critical values of r, α = .10, two-tailed test, df = 14, r = .426; df = 11, r = .476.
* Statistically significant at the .10 level.

little evidence that the advantages of informal education need be lost in the search for "quality."

To make sure that intellectual content and cognitive processes are an integral part of the preschool program does not preclude attainment of other goals. Indeed, it frequently enhances them. If children have plenty of interesting and challenging things to do, conflict is often lessened. If children have severe language problems, an increase in language skills is usually accompanied by a decrease in social and emotional problems.

Can an open educational system effectively incorporate appropriate specific content and enhance appropriate cognitive processes in a situation which also nourishes the child's total development? There is evidence that it can, both from the evaluations and observations reported here and from other programs in the United States and abroad.

Even though evaluation in this program was limited to certain defined areas, it indicated that the children developed trust and confidence in adults and children outside the family to the point where they were able to interact freely even in direct questioning situations. Or perhaps it could more accurately be said that they developed trust and confidence in themselves. Gains were made in knowledge of specific content, but the greatest gains for many children were made in aspects of human behavior which were not measured—enjoyment and success in learning, pride in accomplishment, pleasure in the school situation, increased skill in interpersonal relationships, and so on.

The learning that takes place in these classrooms does not just happen. The teacher's role is still central. The environment is carefully structured and planned not only to meet the children's current interests and needs but also to lead them on to new interests. Planning for the development of problem-solving skills, appropriate concepts, and specific and general language skills in an informal context requires both theoretical and working knowledge about the way young children operate and learn as individuals and in groups. Yet the increased emphasis on early childhood education in the last few years has really answered few of the questions that concern the educator, whose task is to implement the best possible program for the children in his care. There are leads, implications, bits and pieces which seem to fit together—but not quite.

For example, there appears to be fairly general agreement among psychologists, educators, scientists, and mathematicians on both the specific content and the cognitive processes appropriate for emphasis in early childhood programs. However, when explanations are attempted of the relationship between those aspects of knowledge which are best transmitted from one person to another and those ideas which the child is better able to construct for himself, with subtle guidance and "setting up" by the person who is helping him learn, considerable confusion results. Some theorists think these two elements of intellectual functioning—what we can "teach" the child, as contrasted with what the child must "learn"—are relatively independent of each other; others submit that there is no need for the child to go through the laborious work of structuring anything—we can simply tell him; others think that specific content is relatively unimportant—the learning processes are all that matter. Such seemingly theoretical questions are dealt with daily in the classroom. Indeed, it seems as if they are so intertwined that no amount of "teasing" can separate them.

Attempting to make some sense out of the various theories and actually apply them to what is going on in a classroom leads to even more confusion. Take the place of teaching in developing simple number concepts. Certainly the child has to learn number names from someone. I suspect that same someone can also help him learn to use that knowledge to count "things." To say that it is impossible to teach a child the skill of rational counting simply does not correspond with classroom observation. As a matter of fact, the legendary gulf between the child's ability to say the number names in order and his actual ability to count objects was not particularly evident on the counting tasks given the New Nursery School pupils and the middle-class comparison group. And New Nursery School pupils sometimes did better counting objects than they did "just counting."

Many rather definite statements have also been made concerning when children can and cannot do certain things. Unfortunately, these do not always correspond to reality either. For example, in the recognition of various geometric shapes it does seem logical to assume that complex forms, such as a star, would be more difficult for the child to recognize and identify than simple forms, and thus recognition of them would come much later in development. But this is not the case. Probably because of the distinctiveness and familiarity of stars in our culture, most children learn to recognize them quite early—long before the age of five, which is sometimes listed as being typical.

Language and its acquisition force us to look at the teaching-learning question from another viewpoint. Language is, of course, an outstanding example of a portion of culture definitely transmitted from one person to another and would presumably be placed in the "teaching" category. Yet the child plays a far more active role in structuring than most teachers realize. As Carol Chomsky puts it (1969, p. 3), "a child who is acquiring language has the task of constructing for himself a . . . set of rules which will characterize the language that surrounds him and enable him to use it for both speaking and understanding." We may be amused at the child who hears someone speak of, "going to get some booze" and then immediately naïvely asks, "What's a boo?" But that child is exhibiting an excellent grasp of certain grammatical rules of the English language.

Also, current research and theory suggest that in many ways the acquisition of syntax parallels Piagetian theories concerning the development of the child toward adult abilities to understand and reason. That is, there is a regularity and order about the entrance into the child's understanding and expression of many of the syntactical meanings of the language, provided he is interacting with a speaker who uses those meanings. *The key phrase for the teacher, both in language and in other areas of knowledge, seems to be "provided [the child] is interacting."*

In the last few years, curriculum developers and teachers have been attempting to develop materials and experiences to help certain children learn more quickly the language and ideas that most children gradually acquire through a long period of listening and interacting. Careful thinking about the words and the ideas for which they stand is necessary if misconceptions are to be avoided. Often there are many ways, all equally correct, to express an idea either verbally or in action. Often words have multiple meanings and subtleties of meaning which must be considered. Failure to consider these two points can cause confusion and misunderstanding on the part of the child.

For example, vague use of the terms "same," "similar," "alike," "match," "goes with," and "different" will probably result in children who have vague notions about contrasting and comparing. When do we say "big," "bigger," "biggest" and when do we say "little," "middle-sized," and "big"? "Top" and "bottom" are used in a variety of situations, some determined by position and some not. All must be considered. Too often, simplifying to give the "rule" merely imparts partial information or, sometimes, misinformation.

A sensitivity to the language "as she is spoke" is required, plus a theoretical knowledge extensive enough to avoid teaching misconceptions. To help children work toward a more precise yet flexible way of expressing their ideas is a large order, as most teachers are working with only the briefest of guides, which must then be translated into materials and activities for the children.

Current social and economic developments affecting the family unit may also affect a child's acquisition of language. More and more mothers at all income levels are working—some estimates run as high as five out of ten. As a result, more young children are being cared for in groups. Language acquisition in years past has been primarily the result of parent-child interaction. When a child spends most of his waking hours in a group-care situation, what will take the place of the responding, questioning, explaining, answering, and modeling done by the parents? In a group situation will what most mothers do "naturally" have to be done systematically and consciously? Almost certainly it will.

Yet it is by no means evident that language and intellectual development are being stressed in most early childhood centers, much less overstressed. The gap between the concerns of the researcher and developer and what actually goes on in most centers is as great in early education as elsewhere, if not greater.

Additional work needs to be done to help teachers realize the intellectual implications of and language development possibilities in young children's activities—and their responsibilities to plan and interact in those experiences. As the head of an English infant school put it: "If the teacher is not aware of particular aspects of experience, she can't pay attention to them; if she's not aware of the intellectual skills and concepts inherent in the simplest activity, she cannot nourish those skills and concepts in the context of the child's play" (Cazden 1971).

Furthermore, it has been suggested by Hess and Shipman (1968) that the language used can either facilitate or impede understanding and performance. Even the best of teachers will comment on something a child has constructed, painted, drawn, or done with a noninterpretive remark such as: "How nice"; or "That's interesting"; or "You've done a good job." Yet recognition can also be given with a remark that focuses on the intellectual task the child has accomplished, that validates, in a sense, what he has done. "Is your building taller or shorter than I am?" "Is it taller or shorter than you are? . . . Tell me some other things that are taller than you are." The ubiquitous "tell me about it" will not accomplish the same result, at least not until the child has acquired the understanding and use of words with which to label, describe, contrast, and compare. The teacher must help many disadvantaged children learn the words and then provide opportunities for their use in varied situations.

Other critical educational questions arise concerning the best use of limited national and local resources to achieve the goals of early childhood education, especially for children from low-income homes. Such matters involve the number of hours a day in a group, the age at which children begin group participation, and the manner of grouping of young children for care and education. Every solution to these problems presents both advantages and problems to the institutions and people involved.

One of the problems and challenges of family grouping is evident in the evaluations reported in this paper. The deceleration of gain for pupils in the second year of a preschool program, as reported, is not atypical. In fact, some programs which show very high IQ gains in the first year show losses in the second. Some of the reasons for this doubtless revolve around the testing situation itself—the timing of pre- and post-tests, familiarity or lack of familiarity with test materials and testing, and interest or lack of interest in the test. (Overtesting is little discussed, but it is a very real problem in obtaining an accurate estimate of young children's abilities.)

Another possible reason, but not necessarily the easiest to remedy, is that the experiences offered are not challenging enough. Child behavior indicative of this is sometimes observed in the last two or three months of the second year of nursery school.

The experiences offered older prereading children who have been in a group situation for a year or two are often inappropriate, no matter what grouping is used and regardless of the child's socio-economic background. Many of these children are not yet ready for the symbolic work of reading and computation, but have outgrown typical nursery school and kindergarten activities. This is not a new situation. For years some kindergarten teachers have resented nursery schools for producing children who were somewhat bored with kindergarten activities perfectly appropriate for children with no previous group experience. Similarly, children who had been to kindergarten were ready for activities different from those offered children who had not been to kindergarten. With more and more children in group care, the problem must be faced and probably faced earlier.

The answer does not lie with the traditional method of accelerating the rate of progression through activities or subject matter. In the first place, there is no logical end to that.

In addition, many children who are ready for and need "something more" are not necessarily ready to accelerate. They need experiences and explorations in other areas, with other types of learning activities which will help fill in gaps in their knowledge and their basic intellectual skills. There is little material available to bridge the gap—often a chasm—between the type of learning that goes on in most nursery schools and the first semester of kindergarten, and the systematic teaching of reading and computation. Yet such material has been needed for a long time, and the need will increase as children enter group care at earlier ages.

There are many possibilities for further development which might involve explorations in science and mathematics, learning and practicing problem-solving techniques, additional work in comprehending and using grammatical structures appropriate to the child's age, abstract use of language, and activities based on Piaget's theories, as well as broadened experiences with music, literature, and art.

Throughout this discussion there has been an attempt to express the conviction that early childhood education is not a simple matter of enriched experiences, of proper motivation, of "freeing" the children so they can learn, or of finding the kit or manual which tells the teacher exactly what to ask and the child exactly how to respond. Teachers must be educated to be sensitive to the interests and needs of children and their families and then to develop and use programs to meet those needs and the needs of society both now and in the future. There is no simplistic solution to the complicated problem of objectives and methodology for optimal education of young children. The certainties of the early days of the "rediscovery" of early childhood education, led by Head Start and similar programs, have given way to the cold realization that none of us have easy answers to the social, economic, cultural, and educational forces which result in the need for special educational programs for some children. Perhaps our real learning has begun.

REFERENCES

Bellugi-Klima, Ursula. 1968. Evaluating the child's language competence. Urbana, Illinois: National Laboratory on Early Childhood Education.

Caldwell, Bettye, and Soule, David. 1967. *The Preschool Inventory.* Berkeley, California: Educational Testing Service.

Cazden, Courtney B. 1971. Language programs for young children: Notes from England and Wales. In C. B. Lavatelli (ed.), *Preschool language training.* Urbana, Illinois: University of Illinois Press.

Chomsky, Carol. 1969. *The acquisition of syntax in children from 5 to 10.* Research Monograph No. 57. Cambridge, Massachusetts: Massachusetts Institute of Technology Press.

Coopersmith, Stanley. 1967. *The antecedents of self-esteem.* San Francisco, California: Freeman.

Hess, Robert D., and Shipman, V. C. 1968. Early experience and the socialization of cognitive modes in children. In J. S. Frost (ed.), *Early childhood education rediscovered.* New York: Holt, Rinehart & Winston.

Kelly, Edward J., and McAfee, Oralie. 1969. *The New Nursery School research project: October 1, 1968 to September 30, 1969.* Greeley, Colorado: University of Northern Colorado. Contract Number B99–4743, Office of Economic Opportunity.

———. 1970. *The New Nursery School research project: November 1, 1969 to October 31, 1970.* Greeley, Colorado: University of Northern Colorado. Contract Number B00–5086, Office of Economic Opportunity.

McAfee, Oralie. 1968. An oral language program for early childhood. *Promising practices in the teaching of English.* Champaign, Illinois: The National Council of Teachers of English.

———. 1970. Planning the preschool program. *Curriculum is what happens: Planning is the key.* Washington, D.C.: National Association for the Education of Young Children.

McAfee, Oralie, et al. 1969. Task accomplishment inventories. Unpublished manuscript, New Nursery School, University of Northern Colorado, Greeley, Colorado.

Nimnicht, G.; McAfee, Oralie; and Meier, J. 1969. *The New Nursery School.* New York: General Learning Corporation.

TODD RISLEY
University of Kansas
Lawrence, Kansas 66044

IV · SPONTANEOUS LANGUAGE AND THE PRESCHOOL ENVIRONMENT

THE PRESENT GOALS for most preschool intervention programs arose from the observation which led to federal funding for such programs: economically impoverished children enter school academically behind affluent children and are even farther behind when they leave school. The value of these programs was specified in terms of a head start toward school achievement. Their goal was therefore to ensure future school achievement of poverty children at a level comparable to the average of the more affluent society.

This apparently simple and explicit goal is by its very nature an inadequate guide for such programs. The goal is stated in terms of measures which will be realized many years after the intervention is attempted. Reaching that goal would therefore be a matter of good guessing, rare luck, or supernatural vision.

Intelligence tests specifically constructed to correlate with future school achievement are therefore used. These tests allow evaluation shortly after or even during an intervention attempt and thus provide "feedback" for program development. Critical examinations of the test-score changes produced by several years of intervention programs, however, have caused us to question the validity of this test performance "feedback." We see that curriculum content (Weikart 1970) or length of exposure to a program (Gray and Klaus 1970) are not clearly related to observed improvement in test scores, and we see that the pre-test scores have proved to be a far more accurate predictor of future school achievement than the improved post-test scores (Weikart et al. 1970).

Thus, early intervention programs, which were conceived and funded to be a downward extension of formal academic education, have developed without valid feedback as a guide toward their goals. I find it not at all surprising that we are dissatisfied with the results of five years of massive preschool intervention effort. We will go a long way toward improving its performance if we honestly admit that as yet we have no predictors of academic success which can provide valid feedback for evaluating and improving preschool programs.

The Preschool As a Prep School

Most preschool intervention programs have a real or imagined curriculum of lessons, experiences, or activities which purport to teach children skills, concepts, or attitudes which may enable them to achieve in elementary school. The curriculum usually occupies children for three or less hours per day, five or less days per week, and nine or so months per year for one year. Whether this 600-hour "innoculation" can conceivably make the child immune to later educational difficulties, irrespective of his life during the other twenty-one hours of the day, the other days of the week, or the intervening months or years is currently in doubt.

I have found with depressing regularity that skills, attitudes, or concepts last only as long as they are supported. The effect of any specific teaching intervention diminishes as time passes and life goes on. Skills, attitudes, and concepts persist after the teaching has stopped only when there are other identifiable conditions which maintain their continued use and therefore their practice and elaboration.

I suggest that if our objective is primarily one of producing academic success, we should integrate our preschool programs with our neighborhood schools, teaching specifically the skills, attitudes, and concepts which those schools are prepared to maintain. I think that if we did this, the basic nature of a successful "Head Start" program would become clear: not enriched exposure to farms, zoos, and railway stations; not developing concepts of similarities, size, categorization, or conservation; nor even socialization and citizenship—but simply 600 hours of survival training.

SURVIVAL TRAINING IN THE PRESCHOOL

Only a few of the "packaged" preschool programs are obviously oriented toward the first and second grade classroom. Even these only incidentally incorporate survival training which might prepare the children for the forty-pupil first grade with a novice teacher in an old building with bad lighting and dirty restrooms. By survival training I am referring to such skills as sitting quietly, following directions, and speaking clearly; such attitudes as pleasing the teacher, appearing attentive, and shunning troublemakers; and such concepts as "grades," "on time," and "correct."

I have discussed a variety of survival training techniques elsewhere (Risley, Reynolds, and Hart 1970); let me illustrate this point with an example form that paper.

All children need to learn when it is appropriate to talk and when it is appropriate to be silent. This is especially so in a public school setting. We therefore initiated procedures to teach children to talk readily when talking was appropriate and to work silently when talking was inappropriate, as well as to be able to shift quickly between talking and not talking.

A period of the preschool morning in which the children were sitting at tables working on preacademic readiness tasks was the time chosen as most like a public school setting and therefore most appropriate for training. The teachers dispensed snacks and social reinforcement only when the children were talking to other children as they worked. By mid-year the children were talking to each other an average of 30% of the time they were required to spend at the tables completing the readiness tasks. The children were then taught to work quietly without talking to other children; this was done by teachers attending to the children, commenting on their work, and allowing them access to snacks only when they were working quietly. The effects of this procedure—which would be termed Differential Reinforcement of behaviors Other than talking, or DRO—reduced the average time the children spent talking from 30% to approximately 2% of the time (dotted line between days 44–55, Fig. 1).

Following this, one of the tables was designated by the teachers as the talking table simply by placing a large blue box on it. At the talking table the children were reinforced for talking while working, and at the other two tables the children continued to be reinforced for working without talking. Every few days children were seated at different tables until by day 70 all the children had spent several days at both the talking table and the nontalking tables. During this time, the children talked an average of 30% of the time at the talk-

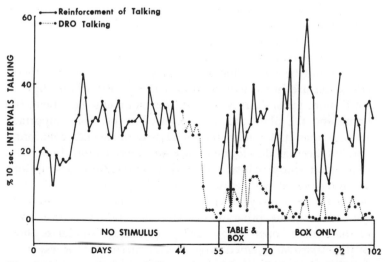

Fig. 1. Average percent of 10-sec. intervals in which each child was observed to be talking. The children were reinforced for talking (*solid line*) or for not talking (*dotted line*).

ing table and an average of 5–10% of the time at the non-talking tables (days 55–70, Fig. 1). Then the children were no longer moved from table to table, but rather the large blue box denoting the talking table was moved to a different one of the three tables every few days. Whenever the box was on their table, and the children were reinforced for talking, they talked to one another an average of 30% of the time. Whenever the box was not on their table and the children were reinforced for working silently, they talked only 1–2% of the time (days 70–92, Fig. 1). Finally the box was moved from table to table every ten minutes during the thirty-minute period each morning, and the children, quickly shifting from talking to working silently, talked to other children 30% of the time when the box was on their table and only 0–5% when it was not (days 92–102, Fig. 1).

Thus we see that whereas it took over seven days for the children to learn to work silently at first, by the end of the year they had complete command of this skill and could immediately respond appropriately to whichever condition occurred. Those programs which are oriented toward the primary school classroom would do well to develop a set of similar specific survival tactics to round out the basic training of their new educational recruits.

It should be noted that many programs of early childhood education are not oriented toward the public school, but toward more general areas of child development. For them, the home and the play yard are professed to be more important settings than the public school classroom. Social, emotional, and intellectual development are considered more important than good study habits, and formal curriculum descriptions are interspersed with explanations of what each activity will do for the self-concept or creative development of the children. Nevertheless, the program descriptions and evaluation tools of these more "open" preschool programs are similar to those of the classroom-oriented programs. A curriculum of lessons or activities is described and data are reported on correlates and predictors of future academic performance.

In brief, we are presently faced with implied or overt competition between various preschool curricula which may have differing theoretical superstructure and may even differ in content. All are implicitly or explicitly attempting to improve the performance of our public schools by innoculating preschoolers against failure.

The validity of this entire endeavor—using preschools as preparatory schools for elementary schools—presupposes that preschools as a whole will be better than our public schools. Whereas I am sure that many preschools are, the vast majority of the public preschool programs in this country are not. Most provide the same image as our urban public schools: lackluster teachers and uninterested (and unruly) children.

Thus, if our objective in preschool is to prepare children to survive and excel in elementary school, we must specifically teach the skills, attitudes, and concepts which elementary schools require and which they will maintain. We must also insure that our preschool programs are even better endowed than our elementary schools and our preschool teachers better prepared.

The Preschool As a Place to live

However, several factors, present and predicted, made *new* objectives in early childhood research imperative. Work training programs, family economics, and feminine equality are producing an exponential rise in day care centers for young children. Day care centers for poor children are being proliferated by the federal government. Fee-supported day care centers, many with programs packaged and franchised by nationwide corporations, are rearing an increasing proportion of our nation's children.

Instead of a short, organized educational interlude in a child's day, as in most intervention preschools, the day care center involves extensive periods of each child's life, including most of his waking hours. The paucity of knowledge of living environments and child-rearing practices appropriate to groups of children, the spectre of the bleak existence of children in most of the residential centers for children currently extant in our society (those for retarded and disturbed children), and the massive, destructive effects attributed to maternal and stimulus deprivation should warn us of severe potential dangers.

To this end we must conduct research to make explicit what is now usually implicit in good programs for young children. We must empirically examine how activities are organized, how materials are selected and presented, and how facilities are designed, so that children are better served in group-care situations. We must establish new goals relating specifically to living environments and child-rearing practices for groups of children, and we must develop new measurement tools and honestly evaluate all programs according to those goals.

Those of us who have been active in developing preschool curricular materials have tended to talk about learning and teaching activities in a preschool as if the children were sitting on a shelf, to be taken down at our convenience and "taught." We have been able to so characterize our preschools because we have had teachers who knew better: teachers who knew that the formal teaching activities we described were a very small part of a preschool program—even a half-day preschool program; teachers who knew that the children spent more time in, and could be more influenced by, the activities which we considered mere "fillers" than in our "curriculum." Most importantly, we have had teachers who knew how to arrange and maintain a setting that would keep groups of children profitably engaged with their physical and social environment throughout the day.

The direction and extent of engagement with the physical and social environment appears to be an almost universal indication of the quality of a living setting for children. Those familiar with preschools and day care centers often evaluate a particular activity area or an entire center at almost a glance, without even knowing the curriculum or the goals of the program, and they usually agree with each other's independent evaluations. They are simply assessing how many of the children are looking at and/or physically interacting with objects or people at any moment in time or, in other words, what proportion of time each child is appropriately engaged with his environment.

Basic to the operation of most preschools is the assumption that in play, when a child concentrates upon a particular object or event for a period of time he gains skill and understanding. Professional preschool teachers are therefore trained to provide, display, and regulate the use of a wide variety of materials and activities in such a way as to maximize the probability of the children's prolonged engagement with them during play.

Thus we find that although unformalized in the preschool literature the tenets of preschool practice provide the outlines of a technology for maintaining a living environment which will engage children in constructive activities. The "Living Environments Group" of the University of Kansas has been active in developing convenient and reliable procedures for measuring the engagement of groups of children with materials, people, and events throughout the day in day care centers. We refer to this set of procedures as the "PLA-CHECK"—*PL*anned *A*ctivity *CHECK*.

After obtaining a schedule of the day's periods and a list of the materials and activities which are provided for the children during each period, a count is made every x minutes of how many children are actually engaged with the materials provided by the teacher at that moment in each area of the preschool. (A complete protocol for the PLA-CHECK is currently being developed and tested in a variety of preschool and day care programs.)

Figure 2 depicts the participation in planned activities throughout an entire day by the children in a subsidized day care center in a poverty neighborhood. We note that after a rather poor morning, during which less than half of the children were participating in planned activities at most PLA-CHECKS, a general improvement was seen during the afternoon. However, when we divide the day to depict each activity area, as at the top of Figure 2, we see that the bulk of the afternoon is occupied by a long nap time, when the chil-

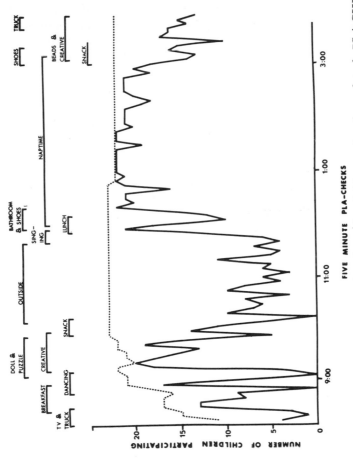

Fig. 2. Total number of children participating in planned activities at the time of each PLA-CHECK spaced five minutes apart throughout the day. Total attendance of three- to five-year-old children during this typical day at this day care center is indicated by the dotted line. The schedule of activities is noted above the graph.

100

dren's participation consists of sleeping. We can also see that the poorest period of the day is the outdoor play period and that there are consistent problems with transitions between activities.

Figure 3 (left) shows the amount of time the day care staff had allocated to each activity during planning. This step alone provides important information upon which to evaluate a program—e.g., it is obvious that no emphasis is placed upon preacademic skills in this day care center. The right portion of Figure 3 indicates the proportion of the day which was devoted to the health-related activities of sleeping, eating, and using the bathroom. Forty-six percent of the day was planned to be devoted to health-related activities; the children, in fact, spent about 46 percent of their time actually engaged in sleeping, eating, and using the bathroom. However, whereas 52 percent of the day was planned to be devoted to preschool activities, the children spent only about 22 percent of their time actually engaged in preschool activities.

We are using this measure to study the effects of various schedules, routines, activities, types of materials, and methods of displaying and presenting materials (LeLaurin and Risley, in press; Doke and Risley, in press). We are continuing to find that our objective data usually confirm the effectiveness of the techniques used by most formally trained preschool teachers. We have also done extensive work on how the materials and events in the free-play periods of a well-organized preschool can then be used to promote particular preacademic skills (Risley 1968; Jacobson, Bushell, and Risley 1969) and maintain a variety of language skills (Reynolds and Risley 1968; Hart and Risley 1968; Risley and Hart 1968; Hart and Risley, in press). Thus we are rapidly proceeding with our program to empirically examine and to formalize the existing technology for maintaining a living environment for groups of toddler and preschool-age children.

For example, a child's spontaneous speech provides a good teacher with day-by-day feedback about the child's social and linguistic progress. Teaching techniques which are described as a teacher's "being sensitive" and "responsive" can be better

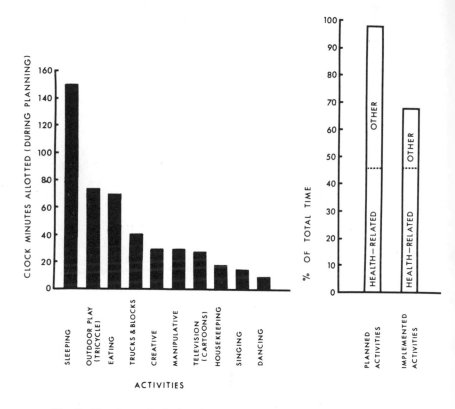

Fig. 3. Number of clock minutes allotted during planning to each activity *(left)*. The percentage of total time planned and implemented has been summarized at *right*. The percentage of total time planned was that in which one or more of the planned activities was actually available to the children. The percentage of total time implemented indicates the average amount of time the children were participating in the planned activities that day.

described and formalized into procedures for elaborating and maintaining spontaneous language.

Over a three-year period the spontaneous speech of four-and-one-half-year-old disadvantaged children has been studied in a typical preschool free-play situation. In the first year of study (see Hart and Risley 1968), it was found that though a group of fifteen children learned to name colors appropriately in a group-teaching situation, color naming did not increase in their spontaneous speech in the nonteaching situation until they were required to name by color the preschool materials which they wanted to use. When access to preschool materials was thus made contingent on use of color-adjective-noun combinations, the rate of such usage increased markedly in the group (see Fig. 4). This effect was replicated the following year with another group of children and other aspects of language (see Hart and Risley, in press); marked increases were seen successively in children's usage of nouns, adjective-noun combinations, and compound sentences when access to preschool materials during free play was made contingent on use of each of these aspects of language in turn (see Fig. 5). In the third year of study we investigated whether spontaneous speech to children as well as to adults could be modified, and we examined the role of teacher prompting in producing the effect. High rates of compound sentence usage in requests for preschool materials were found first directed to teachers and then to children, in accordance with who dispensed the preschool materials during free play. The children's rates of using compound sentences were found to depend only minimally on teacher prompting (see Fig. 6). The conclusions at the end of the three years of investigation are, first, that the materials available in the regular preschool environment can be used to effect important changes in children's behavior and, second, that significant and lasting modifications may be made in specific aspects of the spontaneous speech of disadvantaged children.

Although we rely heavily upon contingent social interaction to develop appropriate behaviors, we must not overlook the possibility that social interaction may function as a reinforcer

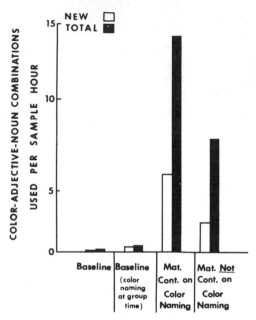

Fig. 4. Average use of color-noun combinations and average rate of appearance of new color-noun combinations per hour of observation in the spontaneous speech of 15 disadvantaged preschool children. The first baseline was from the first to the 102nd day of school. The second baseline was from school days 103 through 152, during which time the children were taught their colors until they could identify, by color, most of the materials and objects in the preschool. Receipt of play materials was made contingent on color naming from school days 153 through 171. From school days 172 through 189 materials were no longer contingent on color naming.

partially because it occasions the assistance of another person in obtaining other reinforcers, and that an important function of language is to guide the other person to efficient assistance. The essence of the use of "natural reinforcers" to elaborate language is to arrange the environment to maximally necessitate the child's obtaining the cooperation and assistance of other people to acquire those reinforcers.

Spontaneous language also provides a means for formal and

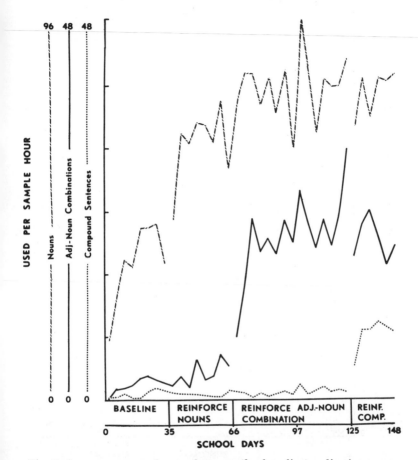

Fig. 5. Average use per hour of nouns (*broken line*), adjective-noun combinations (*solid line*), and compound sentences (*dotted line*) by 12 children across experimental conditions. The experimental conditions were: baseline (days 1–34), access to preschool materials contingent on use of a noun (days 35–65), access to preschool materials contingent on use of an adjective-noun combination (days 66–124), and access to preschool materials contingent on a request in the form of a compound sentence (days 125–148). Note the different scale for nouns versus adjective-noun combinations and compound sentences.

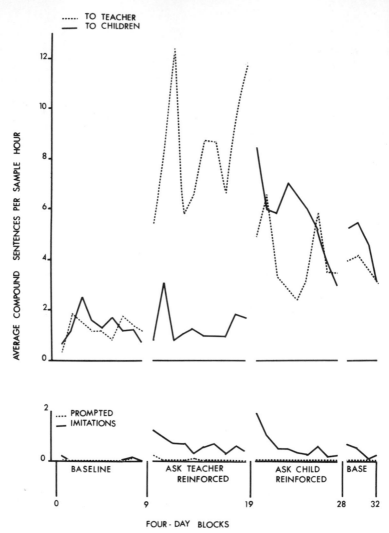

Fig. 6 (Top) Average number of compound sentences directed to a teacher (*dotted lines*) and to other children (*solid lines*) per sample hour over four-day blocks comprising each experimental condition. (*Bottom*) Average number of requests prompted in the form "You need to ask for" or "Why do you want?" (*solid lines*) and in the form of a compound sentence which the child imitated (*dotted lines*). The sequence of experimental conditions was: baseline-free access to materials (blocks 1–9); materials contingent on compound sentence request to teachers (blocks 10–19); and materials contingent on compound sentence request to other children (blocks 20–26).

continuous evaluation of the adequacy of a preschool program in establishing and maintaining language development. The beginnings of a technology for recording spontaneous speech, described by Reynolds and Risley (1968) and Hart and Risley (1968), was a natural outgrowth of earlier language modification research (cf. Risley, Hart, and Doke, in press, for a description of this development). Subsequently, computer programs and data-handling routines were developed which permitted large volumes of transcribed records of spontaneous speech to be analyzed for simpler aspects of language, stored, and easily retrieved and later re-analyzed (Hart 1969; Hart and Risley, in press). This enabled us to closely examine the largely ignored problem in language and linguistic studies—that of interobserver agreement on recording and classifying language.

We were thus able to record and analyze extensive spontaneous language data from a matched group of poverty Negro children enrolled in a Head Start preschool near Juniper Gardens and a comparison group of middle-class children from university families at the University of Kansas Preschool in Lawrence. We could make meaningful comparisons between these groups and the children in our language development program only because we had taken extensive reliability samples among all combinations of observers, recording all children at all settings, and could evaluate the bias in the data attributable to background of observer, acoustics of a setting, etc.

When we compare the spontaneous speech of the children in the three preschools we have a precise picture of the effects of the total language development program at The Turner House Preschool. Figure 7 shows: (*top*) the average total number of words spoken; (*middle*) vocabulary used; and (*bottom*) number of complete sentences per sample each week throughout the school year for each group. These graphs are representative of the patterns shown by the three groups in many other language categories. In general, Head Start children begin the year much lower and gain less during the year than the university children. The children in our Turner House language development program begin the year at the same

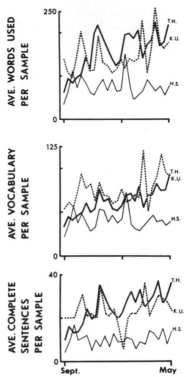

Fig. 7. Comparisons of the average number of words spoken, vocabulary used, and complete sentences formed by children in each of three preschool programs during weekly samples of spontaneous speech. Each child's speech was recorded for 15 minutes during free-play periods once each week throughout the school year. The three groups are: The 12 poverty Negro children in the language development preschool at Turner House (*T.H.*), a matched group of poverty Negro children in a nearby Head Start program (*H.S.*), and 12 children of university professors at the University of Kansas preschools (*K.U.*). Note that the Turner House children began the year similar to the Head Start children and ended the year similar to the professors' children in all three categories of speech.

level as their matched group of Head Start children, but gain most during the year and end the year comparable to the university children.

Like the PLA-CHECK measures, measures of spontaneous

speech allow us to continually monitor our program. We can tell if a child's time is well occupied or wasted, and we can tell whether our preschool or day care center is providing conditions for language practice and language development. Although we cannot now evaluate preschool and day care programs according to later success in public schools, we should evaluate them according to objectives we can measure: objectives as simple—and fundamental—as providing a good place for children to live.

REFERENCES

Doke, Larry A., and Risley, Todd R. The experimental analysis of group care: Activity schedules. *Journal of Applied Behavior Analysis*, in press.

Gray, Susan W., and Klaus, Rupert A. 1970. The early training project: A seventh year report. *Child Development* 41: 909–24.

Hart, Betty M. 1969. Investigations of the language of disadvantaged preschool children. Doctoral dissertation, University of Kansas.

Hart, Betty M., and Risley, Todd R. 1968. Establishing use of descriptive adjectives in the spontaneous speech of disadvantaged preschool children. *Journal of Applied Behavior Analysis* 1: 109–20.

———. The use of preschool materials for modifying the language of disadvantaged children. *Journal of Applied Behavior Analysis*, in press.

Jacobson, J. M., Bushnell, D., and Risley, Todd R. 1969. Switching requirements in a Headstart classroom. *Journal of Applied Behavior Analysis* 2: 43–47.

LeLaurin, Kathryn, and Risley, Todd R. The organization of day care environments: The "zone defense" versus the "man-to-man defense." *Journal of Applied Behavior Analysis*, in press.

Reynolds, N. J., and Risley, Todd R. 1968. The role of social and material reinforcers in increasing talking of a disadvantaged preschool child. *Journal of Applied Behavior Analysis* 1: 253–62.

Risley, Todd R. 1968. Learning and lollipops. *Psychology Today*, January.

Risley, Todd R., and Hart, Betty H. 1968. Developing correspondence between the non-verbal and verbal behavior of preschool children. *Journal of Applied Behavior Analysis* 1: 267–81.

Risley, Todd R., Hart, Betty M., and Doke, Larry A. Operant language development: The outline of a therapeutic technology. *The language of the mentally retarded.* U.S. Government Printing Office, in press.

Risley, Todd R., Reynolds, N. J., and Hart, Betty M. 1970. Behavior modification with disadvantaged preschool children. In R. Bradfield (ed.), *Behavior modification: The human effort.* Palo Alto, California: Science and Behavior Books.

Weikart, David P. 1970. A comparative study of three preschool curricula. In J. Frost (ed.), *Disadvantaged child* (2nd ed.). New York: Houghton Mifflin.

Weikart, David P., Deloria, Dennis J., Lawser, Sarah A., and Wiegerink, Ronald. 1970. *Longitudinal results of the Ypsilanti Perry Preschool Project.* Ypsilanti, Michigan: High/Scope Educational Research Foundation.

MARION BLANK
Albert Einstein College of Medicine
Bronx, N.Y. 10461

V · THE TREATMENT OF PERSONALITY VARIABLES IN A PRESCHOOL COGNITIVE PROGRAM*

IN THE PAST DECADE, child development research has shifted its emphasis from psychodynamic to cognitively oriented formulations. Those who have worked with the disadvantaged have been among those most ready to adopt this new orientation, since learning problems seem paramount in these children. The shift from affect to cognition can be only relative, however. The problems of the disadvantaged are largely those of applied research—in particular, the development of effective educational programs. The demands of reality force such programs to deal (implicitly, if not explicitly) with both affect and cognition, if they are to have any hope of success. But the shift has clearly taken place, as witnessed by the fact that many compensatory programs define their key variables almost solely within a cognitive frame of reference (Bereiter and Engelmann 1966; Gahagan and Gahagan 1971; Karnes et al. 1970; Weikart and Weigerink 1968).

My own work in this area has been marked by a similar focus (Blank and Solomon 1968, 1969; Blank 1970). Like many investigators, I am convinced that disadvantaged children are seriously hampered by cognitive deficiencies. Nevertheless, I

* This work was supported by USPHS grants No. MH08498 and MH17904, the Ford Foundation, and the Grant Foundation. The author wishes to express her appreciation to the day care centers and the New York City public schools for their excellent cooperation in this research.

believe that we have underestimated the significance of affective variables in compensatory preschool education. The affective variables to which I refer do not relate to general patterns of emotional development in the young child (e.g., the Oedipal situation, sibling rivalry, need for security, etc.). They refer, instead, to factors that are specifically associated with the disadvantaged child's difficulty with cognition.

The situation in brief is as follows: The disadvantaged child has widespread, serious learning problems; the compensatory program is established to overcome these difficulties. Although this may seem like a logical, beneficial development, it actually contains the potential for serious conflict. It is the adult and not the child who sees the compensatory program as helpful. The child sees it only as a situation in which he is required to do all the things that he is least capable of doing. From his point of view he only stands to lose, since his weaknesses are bound to be exposed. As a result, he does his utmost to remove himself from this situation, since it is one that makes him uncomfortable and insecure. In other words, the disadvantaged child is geared toward avoiding those situations which the educational program is specifically designed to foster.

The child need not be consciously aware of his anxiety.* His experience is simply that people—even people he may like—are demanding "something" from him and he does not understand what that something is. Cognitive demands, even when made in a seemingly interesting and supportive way, can thus serve to trigger a variety of defenses—including withdrawal, anger, resistance, and denial. As is well known, these are typical reactions to stress situations in all children, regardless of stratum. What is being proposed here, however, is that the learning situation itself can be a major source of stress, especially for the child who experiences difficulties in the intellectual sphere.

If the situation is as serious as this, the question naturally

---

* In our experience, however, such awareness has been clearly present by five years of age.

arises: "How could we have avoided recognition of the problem for so long?" The answer lies in the structure of most preschool education. The present-day nursery school represents the culmination of a long history of effort on the part of leaders such as Montessori (1912) and Froebel (1896). The structure that they evolved is a comfortable one that meets many of the social and emotional needs of the young child. There are games to play with, activities to indulge in, friends to speak to, and routines to go through. This predictable, pleasant structure is as appealing to the disadvantaged child as it is to most other groups of children.

All these positive aspects do not necessarily lead the child to learn. In fact, the group-based structure of nursery school helps protect the child in his efforts to avoid learning. Because so many other children are present, the child has opportunities for "appropriately" completing an activity even when he is totally unaware of the cognitive content of the task. This can occur through imitation, habit, or rote associations. For example, many children happily join in group singing by uttering nonsense syllables in place of the words of the song. The presence of fifteen other voices that are singing the appropriate words easily disguises the child's failure. The traditional group-based nursery school situation is thus perfectly designed to perpetuate the avoidance of learning in those children who have the most difficulty in learning. (The situation, of course, changes markedly once elementary school begins. The child is then required to show skill in areas such as reading and arithmetic. The group, though present, no longer serves to cloak his ignorance. As a result, his emotional reactions against the pressures of the learning situation become inescapably apparent.)

These factors may help explain why the heavily cognitive Bereiter–Engelmann program (1966) was among the first compensatory programs to give explicit consideration to affective variables. This situation may seem paradoxical in view of the frequent criticisms of the program as one which fails to consider the children's emotional needs. The break with the usual nursery school format, however, is precisely why it had to deal with emotional factors. Unlike the much more free-flowing large group situation, it used small, structured groups in which responses were demanded of the children. Once responses were demanded, failures to respond (whether through fear or recalcitrance) had to be dealt with specifically. Their approach to the problem is indicated in the broad principles they outline for dealing with "troublesome," "withdrawn," and "indifferent" children (pp. 88–90).

The work described below also stems from a preschool program which departed from the traditional group structure. The program, which is one that I have been developing, is based on a daily fifteen-minute tutorial session designed to foster the precursors of abstract thinking in the preschool age (three through five years) disadvantaged child (Blank and Solomon 1968, 1969; Blank 1970). The tutorial setting was selected as a means of giving the teacher the control needed both to continually diagnose the child's difficulties and readjust the lesson to make it appropriate to the child's level. The child is led through a Socratic-type dialogue to develop cognitive skills (e.g., selective attention, inner verbalization, ability to delay, imagery of future events, etc.) that will lay the foundation for strategies of thinking and information processing.

These goals cannot be attained, even in a one-to-one setting, if the child's resistance to learning is not overcome. The techniques thus far developed represent our preliminary endeavors in this regard. Unfortunately, this aspect of the work is less well theoretically grounded than the cognitive aspect of the program. In many cases, the broad guidelines simply represent educated trial-and-error guesses that we have found to be helpful. Ideas for dealing with the disturbed child in the classroom setting (see Hewett 1968; Peter 1965) have also proven helpful, although they have had to be altered considerably because of the factors of age (the preschool vs. the school age child) and setting (a one-to-one as opposed to a group teaching setting). The formulations presented below will almost certainly be revamped as the work progresses. Nevertheless, it is hoped that they will serve as a useful beginning for discussion of this problem.

Before proceeding to our guidelines, it is worth while to consider the basic goals of any treatment program, for these goals ultimately dictate much of the basic methodology that will be adopted. All intervention is naturally directed toward helping the individual function more effectively. But this goal can be achieved in a number of different ways.

1. The deficit can be attacked directly by making the person engage in the activity with which he is having difficulty. This approach is widely used with nonorganic disorders (e.g., reading retardation and phobias), but it is adopted for certain organic difficulties as well. For example, attempts to teach deaf children to speak and comprehend vocal language are based on this philosophy. Generally, this approach employs techniques similar to programmed learning in that the demands on the person are slowly but progressively increased. This approach represents the goal not only of the tutorial program but of almost all compensatory education for the disadvantaged child. The training is designed to allow him to develop the same skills that the advantaged child is deemed to possess.

2. The deficit can be by-passed through the development of compensatory devices (i.e., by developing alternative skills which are available in the organism). This approach is most common with organic malfunctions such as blindness and deafness, but it may exist in other spheres as well. For example, one adult dyslexic who was the president of an engineering company reported that he had so arranged his life through the use of tape recorders, excellent secretaries, and an acute memory that the demands for him to read would be almost nonexistent. This goal is generally strongly rejected for the disadvantaged child, since it is felt that it would leave him in a permanently inadequate state.

3. The difficulty may be channeled so that it becomes a point of strength. This approach requires that the environment be engineered so that the difficulty is now an advantage. This is a rare occurrence since, by definition, there are few opportunities in which undesirable behavior is desirable. Nevertheless, such opportunities can be created. For instance,

a child's bossiness can be turned to advantage by making him captain of the class. The hope in these cases, naturally, is not to reinforce the maladaptive behavior, but rather to place it in a setting where the behavior is both controlled and accepted. It is then hoped that the secondary reward of approval will serve as an impetus to help the child readapt his style of coping with the world.

As stated above, the tutorial program is directed toward the first goal. Our work has indicated that children who are reached by the age of three or four can successfully master higher level cognitive skills. After this age, however, entrenched error patterns, unthinking rote behaviors, and deeply ingrained fear of failure make the desired changes increasingly difficult to bring about.

While the second and third goals do not represent the ultimate aim of the teaching, they need not be discarded at all points in the teaching. Each of these goals has served useful roles, particularly in the initial stages of instruction. The early stages pose the greatest difficulty for the child, since it is a time when he has the fewest skills and the greatest fears. Any techniques which will help him to overcome this trying period should be considered.

The child's personality largely determines which goals will be adopted. For example, attempts to make the withdrawn child engage in the activities in which he is deficient (goal 1) only serve to reinforce his anxiety and withdrawal. He must first gain confidence in himself. To this end, the second goal is most useful, since it allows the child to rehearse those skills in which he is proficient. Once some measure of security is attained, the child can then be placed in situations which require him to develop skills in which he is deficient. By contrast, the third goal is most useful in the initial work with the hyperactive child. His constant urge for action is called into play, but under controlled conditions. Control of his activity is prerequisite for the development of almost any other cognitive skills. Thus, affective variables strongly influence the pacing and selection of the teaching. It is hoped that the discussion that follows will clarify the exact nature of this relationship. The major personality types to be considered here are: (1) the hyperactive child; (2) the shy, withdrawn child; (3) the verbally facile child; and (4) the negativistic child.

THE HYPERACTIVE CHILD

While excessive motor activity is often common in these children, the most basic difficulty is in their mental hyperactivity. Their minds, like butterflies, skip so rapidly from one thing to another that it seems impossible to capture their attention. As the teacher attempts to organize some material, the child grabs at one thing and then another, frequently chattering away with unrelated comments such as: "I got that"; "Oh, let's play with this"; "My mommy is gonna buy me one of these"; and "Joey is sick today." In marked contradiction to the stereotype of the silent, averbal disadvantaged child, their words pop out freely but also thoughtlessly, so that their speech often creates a barrier to learning. In the group setting the child's difficulties lead to a frustrating pattern of interaction between the child and the teacher. The former indulges in his usual uncontrolled activity, while the latter punishes, cajoles, or threatens in varied attempts to establish control.

Once their difficulties are overcome, these children are among the most delightful to work with. The energy that propelled the hyperactivity is now available to create a lively zest for learning. The problem, of course, is "How does one exert effective control?" The hyperactive child's predominant characteristic is a rapid succession of intense, but logically unconnected, bits of behavior. The child is attracted to a toy—so he runs to it; on his way, he sees a different toy and decides to take that instead; after a moment he drops it and looks for something else; and so on ad infinitum. There is one major advantage to this uncontrolled stream of actions—although the endless change is difficult to bear, each response by itself is generally quite reasonable and readily available.

Because these are reasonable behaviors, they can be used as stepping stones to a more advanced cognition. For this purpose, pace is vital; a stream of commands is given in rapid fashion so that the child is impelled to follow the verbally directed action and has little time to be drawn to irrelevancies. For example, the teacher may say to the child that she needs some crayons and make the simple request, "Get me the crayons over there." Immediately after the child returns she can say, "Oh, I forgot to ask for paper. Run and get the paper." Again upon the child's return she can issue a host of commands like: "Oh, the door isn't closed. Better close it fast before we sit down"; or "I think there are some better crayons in the other cabinet. Bring them, too." The focus on action-based commands suits the child well. He is both happy with the action and disarmed by this method as heretofore these same behaviors were the basis of much adult-child antagonism.

This method contrasts with techniques commonly used by behaviorists in classroom management problems. The latter stress self-inhibition of motor behavior by the child through rewarding him for any time period in which a negative behavior is not emitted. By contrast, the action-based techniques of the tutorial program allow the child to engage in his normally disruptive motor behavior—but in such a way that the behavior is subtly controlled by an external authority figure. The goal is not for the child to develop immediate internalization of control, but rather to help him establish a relationship whereby the adult is seen as nonantagonistic, even though controlling. It is hereby proposed that the child will be incapable of learning what is available from the mature, adult world if this type of relationship is not established.

After some initial control has been established, impulsivity can be further controlled through delay, e.g., "Wait, before you go, tell me what I asked you to bring." Gradually, tasks can be introduced that demand greater concentration and effort (e.g., "Okay, now let's sit down and put this puzzle together."). The child will comply with these demands if they do not dominate the lesson and if he is given a desired reward for completing the distasteful task, e.g., "As soon as you finish the puzzle you can have the flashlight that you told me you wanted to play with."

American educational philosophy has hotly debated the issue of material rewards, since they are deemed to conflict with the avowed goal of "learning for learning's sake." The merits and disadvantages of the reward system are beyond the scope of this presentation. Suffice it to say that we have found material rewards to be useful in the initial stages of teaching the hyperactive child. The rewards are self-selected in that the teacher offers only those objects which the child clearly values. In addition, they are offered only after a sequence of activity, when the child has completed the work set out for him. Within two or three weeks, material rewards can generally be dispensed with, since the child's growing skills lead him to value the material for its intrinsic rewards. With all this, the greatest satisfaction is obtained from the opportunity for rapid movement. Compared to this, the extrinsic rewards are relatively minor.

These considerations about rewards may appear to be similar to the conditioning techniques commonly in use in classroom management problems. While there are similarities, there are also differences. First, the rewards in the tutorial program are much less obvious than in typical conditioning procedures (Risley and Hart 1968). For example, there is nothing comparable to a signal box wherein the child receives specific tokens (e.g., a marble) whenever he emits the desired behavior. Instead, the reward is frequently an integral part of the cognitive problem. Thus, in a lesson to be described below, the reward was the opportunity for the child to take some pudding back with him to his class. To this end, he was willing to respond to a lengthy and quite impressive list of cognitive demands. Second, because they are bound up with the content of the lesson, the reinforcements in the tutorial setting are much more variable. To the extent that the lesson changes, so do the reinforcements change. For example, in a lesson on food, the reward might be eating the final product; in a lesson on a ball, the reward might be rolling the ball. In each case the reward is granted because the child has complied with relevant cognitive demands concerning these objects. This situation contrasts to the signal box, where the reward is highly consistent from one session to the next. Third, the constant interweaving of the dialogue situation makes it possible to introduce much more flexibility between the presentation of a demand and the attainment of the reward. Thus, if the teacher notes that the child is functioning well, she may introduce one or two more demands before actually giving the reward. Conversely, if the child is extremely restless, the reward may be given more quickly.

These comments may make it appear as though we are rewarding negative behaviors and punishing positive behaviors (i.e., a child seems to get fewer external rewards when he is performing better). In one sense, this generalization is true, since the better functioning the child the less the need for external rewards. In another sense, however, the generalization is an inaccurate representation of the situation. The child is never given the reward until the specific act is completed. Therefore, he does not perceive the situation as one where he has "gotten away with something." In addition, the reward is generally the very material being discussed; as a result, it possesses a different kind of meaning than in most conditioning situations. Greater or lesser ease in obtaining the reward is not seen as reward or punishment, but much more, as the give-and-take of any normal discussion. This allows rewards to be phased out more readily, since the positive aspect of the reward is readily transferred to the entire tutorial dialogue. Rewards, however, are never totally absent, since the child must have the opportunity to enjoy what he is doing or he will not do it. The balance between work (cognitive effort) and reward rapidly shifts to favor work. Intrinsic motivation becomes the reward as the child recognizes the power of cognition in helping him grapple with the world.

These differences between rewards in the tutorial setting and in the traditional conditioning paradigms would seem to be significant. Nevertheless, both methods may be equally effective in modifying behavior to some desired end. This matter can be settled only by research directed toward the comparison of different reinforcement principles.

Even aside from the issue of rewards, the early tutorial sessions stand in contradistinction to the later ones. First, the sessions may be short; they may last for as little as five minutes. The duration is determined by the child's initial level of functioning. Once there are marked signs of fatigue or inattention, continuation of the lesson will only reinforce the child's patterns of distraction. Nevertheless, it is advisable to keep the child working for about one or two minutes longer than he wishes. This can be done by rewards ("As soon as you finish this last one, you can take it with you.") or by rapid pacing, since this rarely fails to capture the child's impulsivity ("Oh, good, we're almost finished. But look, if you hurry, we can still finish this last one. Come on, work as fast as you can.").

Second, the initial sessions lack meaningful development of a theme. By contrast, later lessons are almost always characterized by the sustained, sequential examination of a set of material. The hyperactive child would not tolerate such detailed analysis and concentration in the initial teaching. Instead, he is given a group of unconnected, action-based commands that are joined by a thin veneer of content (e.g., in one session, most of the items might be tangentially related to the task of playing ball). The major goal is to have the child control his behavior so that it is in line with the demands of another person. This adaptation is prerequisite to any meaningful teaching.

Third, the child's extensive skills of expressive verbalization are relatively ignored. When a child speaks freely, there is a strong temptation to ask questions which tap these skills (e.g., "What did you do in school today?", "What did you see on the trip with your class?", etc.). Despite their wide verbal repertoire, these children frequently do not grasp the meaning of the words they use. They are the masters of the irrelevant comment. For example, when asked "Why do you use chalk to write on the blackboard?" one child replied, "To make you big and strong." Questions that demand expressive verbalization thus reinforce the child's random, irrelevant comments. As a result, most of the initial teaching effort is directed toward having the child learn to be receptive to the verbalization of others (receptive language) and to begin to use brief expressive verbalization in a precise manner.

Fourth, inadequate performance is clearly judged as unacceptable. For example, if a child draws a rough blob when he was asked to "draw a square," the teacher might say "No, that's not a good square." The child will then be made to repeat the task until it is accomplished correctly. If the child's performance indicates that the task is too demanding for him, the demands can be reduced without making any specific comment about the simplification. For example, in re-presenting the task to the child, the teacher may draw three of the sides and simply ask the child to complete the fourth. The child should be left with the feeling that adequate completion of the task is expected and that continued poor performance will be self-defeating.

It is for this reason that reward is needed. The child is confronted with tasks which require him to exert unaccustomed effort and care. He sees no reason for the compliance unless he feels that the desired behavior is worth while. For example, one hyperactive boy was eager to blow out the candles on a cake. The teacher used this wish to serve as the reward for the child's completing a series of interposed acts demanding imitation, control, and delay. She said that he could blow out the candles if he said "1, 2, 3, blow" (intentionally, the simpler number sequence of 1, 2, 3, was complicated by adding the word "blow" since the child could shout out the number sequence without thought). The child responded happily, said "1, 2, 3," looked abashed and said, "I forgot the other thing." The teacher then blew out the candles and explained to the child that because he didn't complete the task correctly, he could not do it "this time."

If the situation had been concluded at that point, the effect might have been disastrous. It would merely have reinforced the child's feeling that effort was in vain. Instead the teacher said, "I'll give you another chance." As she relit the candles and repeated the demands, the child listened attentively. He then proceeded to complete the task correctly. The situation is thus structured to provide as much help as the child needs to complete the task successfully. He is never left to struggle with the hopelessness of failure. At the same time, however, he is not permitted to leave the task until he has completed it correctly. Because of the child's difficulty in concentration, he is given no more than one or two demanding tasks in any one session. The remainder of the lesson is devoted to the exercise of less demanding (but nevertheless directed) tasks which the child can complete with little strain.

THE SHY, WITHDRAWN CHILD

The withdrawn child presents a markedly different picture from the hyperactive child. The major goal with the hyperactive child is the control of his explosive activity; the major goal with the withdrawn child is a careful probing until a response is finally elicited. Nevertheless, the initial lessons for both types of children share an emphasis on motor activity. The purpose and structure of the activity, however, is different in each case. With the hyperactive child, teacher-directed activity is introduced to prevent the uncontrolled activity that would occur if the child were left to his own devices. With the withdrawn child, motor activity is used because it is among the least demanding behaviors. Therefore, it provides the child with a nonthreatening task that he can complete correctly. In many cases, the request must even be reduced to the level of simple imitation. Occasionally, the teacher may actually guide the child's movements to effect the desired action (e.g., if the child refuses to pick up a cup, the teacher may put the child's hands on the cup saying, "Let's do it together").

In sharp contrast to the hyperactive child, almost any response should be accepted; if it is anywhere near the goal, it should be praised. Total refusal to comply, however, should not be accepted. It is typical of withdrawn children to show massive inhibition of activity when under stress. In the learning situation, this emerges as a general lack of response. Their most effective defense is simply to be silent in the face of cognitive demands. The silence is amazingly effective. Nothing is more disconcerting than to talk with a person who refuses to participate. One's typical reaction is to feel compassion for the child's ostensible fragility and to withdraw in the face of futile efforts at interchange. The silence protects the child for the moment, but it allows his pattern of withdrawn nonlearning to become even more firmly ingrained. In effect, the child trains the teacher to become as silent with him as he is with her (instead of the hoped-for opposite outcome). For example, teachers frequently lower their voices to a whisper when they are with these children, in an apparent effort to allay the child's anxiety. This procedure not only reinforces the child's pattern of whispering but the message itself is often lost because of the disadvantaged child's difficulties in auditory discrimination (Deutsch 1966).

The resistance may be overcome if the teacher adopts the somewhat bizarre role of pretending that it does not exist. This pose is most effective when combined with attractive, nonthreatening play materials that lower the child's resistance to participation. The well-known materials of water, food, dolls, and doll houses are particularly suitable, for the child is drawn to manipulate the objects. During the child's activity, the teacher confidently chatters away as if all were well. The child's comfort with the material and the teacher's undemanding presence takes the child off guard, since he is not prepared for this situation. During her monologue, the teacher begins to make simple requests in a matter-of-fact way; the command qualities of language almost propel the child to carry out the action. For example, the child may be washing a doll and the teacher may say, "Oh, she's been in the water so long. Let's get her dry. See the towel over there. I think we could use that."

Once the child has executed several commands correctly, the teacher may slip in some demands for expressive verbalization (e.g., "Oh, the doll is wet. You say wet." or "What did we say the doll's name was?"). The requests for expressive verbalization should seem like incidental after-thoughts; should they stand out as focal demands the child's resistance will immediately be raised. Any refusal to respond by the child should be treated casually, as if it were of no import. Despite the seeming nonchalance, however, the teacher should be alert to the child's every refusal. Once a particular type of demand has been refused (e.g., a demand for expressive verbalization, a demand for memory, etc.) a similar type of demand should not be posed in that session. Unless the child's behavior indicates that a major change has occurred, the same refusal is almost bound to occur. The teacher must therefore be alert to every cue emitted by the child. These cues should not be explicitly acknowledged, interpreted, or discussed (e.g., one should not say "I understand, you don't want to talk now"), since this focuses attention on them and thereby reinforces their existence. The cues emitted by the child, however, strongly influence the teacher's subsequent responses.

Extrinsic rewards are almost never used with these children, since they are often too fearful to be willing to accept them. For example, many of these children refuse candy when it is offered. They act as if there were some booby trap accompanying the candy. Even if the candy is accepted it is rarely sufficient to encourage a withdrawn child to do what he is fearful of doing. Instead, these children are much more responsive to signs of their own accomplishments. They are extremely unsure of themselves and can face only those situations which have almost no potential for failure. In effect, their reward is the absence of failure and its subsequent humiliations. This goal requires that the child be presented with many simple tasks in which he is bound to succeed.

As withdrawn children begin to gain confidence, they frequently enter the famous negative stage of the typical two-year-old child. A request such as "Let's draw" may be met not by cowed silence, but by a firm "No, I don't want to." While it is tempting to speculate about the significance of the negativism (e.g., the need to test out the teacher's love, the need to repeat a stage that was inadequately dealt with earlier, etc.), for teaching purposes the most central issue revolves about the effective management of the response. Once the negative response occurs, we have found it useful to honor it but not to emphasize it. For example, if the child refuses to get some crayons that the teacher requests, the teacher can say, "I'll get them and, in the meantime, you put the puzzles away."

The most effective treatment, however, is to design the situation so that the negative response is possible but not probable. This entails the elimination of questions permitting yes–no responses (e.g., "Do you want to play this game?") and the inclusion of open-ended questions which contain the expectation that the child will make a definite choice ("Which of these games do you want to play with today?"). It is also useful to avoid lengthy introductory periods at the beginning of each lesson (e.g., casual conversation about the day's activities before the actual teaching begins). By moving rapidly into the core of the lesson, the child becomes caught up with the content and there is a consequent decline in the negative response.

Perhaps, the most effective way to reduce the negative response is to allow the child to engage in games involving aggression and physical force. As might be expected from analytic theory, these children show a strong attraction to aggressive behavior once their initial fear is lessened. They like games where they can punch objects, knock down toys, and so on. It is generally both threatening to the child and defeating of cognitive goals to permit the child simply to engage in these activities in an undirected way. Instead, the game can be incorporated within a cognitive context in which relevant ideas are explored. For example, the child may play a simplified version of bowling, in which he must follow directions ("This time try to knock down the end one"), describe his behavior ("Which ones did you hit that time?"), and use relevant concepts ("How many pins did you pick up?"). With this type of cognitive structure, the child's aggression is controlled and his intellectual mastery is increased. When the withdrawn child is capable of dealing with this situation, his lessons need no longer depart from those that are given to less fearful children.

It is difficult to estimate the percentage of hyperactive and shy children among the disadvantaged preschool population, for the numbers vary according to ethnic group, the neighborhood, and so on. Nevertheless, both types are common and it is not rare to find a majority of the children falling into one or another of these groups. By contrast, the group to be discussed below—the verbally facile child—is rare among the disadvantaged, but often found among poorly functioning middle-class children. Nevertheless, it is important to recognize the presence of this type of child among the disadvantaged, for, as described below, his weaknesses are often viewed as strengths.

THE VERBALLY FACILE CHILD

This type of child is one who wears a mask of verbal skills which protects him from having to deal with the concrete (physical) world. Often he has mastered details the adult world deems important, such as his birth date, his address, and his father's occupation. His seeming verbal proficiency is no cause for concern since many well-functioning children possess comparable information. The verbosity becomes a source of concern only when it is accompanied by major inadequacies in other spheres, such as perceptual skills (e.g., puzzles).

The disadvantaged children whom we have seen in this group commonly come from overprotective, upwardly mobile homes. For example, one such child in our project was raised by an elderly grandmother who desperately wanted the child to succeed in school. She laboriously taught him details which she deemed vital to school, such as writing his name at four years of age. His conversation and manner were like those of a miniature adult. In contrast to his fluent speech, he was reluctant to manipulate material, especially objects that required large (gross) motor movements (e.g., playing ball).

Verbal memory is often highly developed in these children, for they "get by" by absorbing everything they hear. Should their memorized information prove insufficient, however, these children seem to become paralyzed. They are hesitant about taking a guess, since they cannot tolerate the possibility of error. They become immobilized when having to deal with the unknown. For example, one little girl readily answered questions about the purpose of a shoe (e.g., "We wear them on our feet") and its composition ("It's made of leather")—facts she already knew. When asked, however, about the previously unnoticed laces she would not venture any response. The resistance did not simply concern information which she could not be expected to determine (e.g., the label "shoe lace" could not be achieved if she had not been taught the name); it extended even to information which she could have thought through by herself (e.g., the function of the shoe laces). For example, she recognized that the laces were attached to the shoes. Yet when asked "What do you think will happen if we take this part [the lace] out of the holes?", she attempted no answer. When the teacher executed the action and showed that the shoe fell off, the child's facial expression suggested that she had no inkling of the answer before this point (or could not permit herself the privilege of contemplating such "unacceptable" actions).

This example is typical of the difficulty these children have with imagery of future events. In contrast to their ready verbalization of the already known, imagery demands that they go beyond the secure, immediate present. They generally recoil against this demand and wait until the requested information is supplied by someone else. They also retreat from manipulation of objects, since it carries with it a high possibility of error. This deficiency is apparent in their poor handling of puzzles, drawing, and perceptual sequencing.

The great difficulty in working with these children is in developing their motivation to learn. Unlike hyperactive and withdrawn children, these children already possess a repertoire of skills that seems to go a long way in the adult world. Fearing failure, they feel they can only lose if they attempt to handle unknown materials.

One possible source of motivation is to introduce another child into the tutorial sessions. The presence of another child reduces the child's anxiety about possible errors, since he is not the only one to face failure. In addition, many of these children are friendless because their behavior is so incongruent with the motoric orientation of the typical preschool child. Thus, the presence of another child offers the possibility of friendship. (This arranged situation is markedly different from the traditional classroom grouping. Even though many children are theoretically available in the group, this child remains alone and lonely.)

The second child should be one who is more willing to comply with demands for action and physical manipulation. His compliance encourages the verbally facile child to attempt these behaviors. If the facile child has difficulty in carrying out the behaviors he fears, the teacher should be prepared to demonstrate them. For example, in the shoe lace lesson above, when the child refused to take the shoe lace out of the shoe (in sharp contrast to the glee with which a hyperactive child would carry out such an activity) the teacher first executed the request herself and then reverted to cognitive demands by asking the child "What happened to the shoe?"

This approach is useful with sequences in which observation can be as effective as manipulation (e.g., watching an event and then reporting on it). It is not useful with problems of spatial relationships (e.g., puzzles) where the bulk of the problem resides directly in the manipulation of the parts. Because this area tends to be anxiety provoking, it is useful to design each lesson so that these difficult problems are dealt with for two or three minutes within each lesson. If they are allowed to occupy more time than this, they will unduly increase the child's anxiety and resistance.

THE NEGATIVISTIC CHILD

The negativistic child would seem at first to represent a more extreme version of the hyperactive or the withdrawn child. Closer inspection, however, reveals a much greater pathology which goes far beyond the cognitive stresses of the school setting. In many ways, these children typify Redl's term "Children Who Hate" (1957). In large measure, their primary problems are not cognitive but interpersonal. Since cognitive demands largely occur within an interpersonal context, however, serious cognitive problems arise as a result of their emotional difficulties. Their outstanding characteristic is a tremendous amount of negativistic behavior, including tantrums, destructive breaking of objects, anger, and marked resistance to learning. For example, one of the children in our study showed positive affect only in relationship to the topic of death. In contrast to her usual anger and violence, she burst gleefully into the room one day because she had "found a dead bird outside." This behavior was not an isolated incident, but instead repeated itself in varying forms over the course of the year.*

The existence of such deep pathology naturally leads one to feel that the only proper course of action is referral to a psychiatric service. While this course is highly desirable, it often does not exist as a viable option, since facilities for adequate psychological care are extremely limited, particularly in neighborhoods where the disadvantaged children live. In addition, in some of the studies we were simply assigned children on the basis of their poor test performance. Because of the controlled nature of the research, we were not permitted to "drop" children once the study had begun. We were thereby faced with the need to adapt the tutorial program so that it might be helpful to these children as well.

Because of the great variability in their behavior, we found it essential to treat each child in a totally different manner. Fortunately, the percentage of such children is small, making detailed individual diagnosis more feasible. In marked contrast to the "average disadvantaged child" for whom cognitive effort was worth while because it carried with it the attention and responsivity of an interested adult, the one factor that seemed to be shared by negativistic children was a fear of entering into a relationship with the adult. At best, they had great ambivalence about the relationship with an adult. There

---

* This is not to be interpreted to mean that the child was truly happy when close to the issue of death and destruction, but rather to provide a graphic example of the type of behavior that may occur.

are usually some vestiges of a desire for this relationship—the child is generally quite willing to go with the teacher for most of the sessions; but once in the room, his negativism and hostility becomes evident. He acts as if the driving force of his life was self-destructive anger. For example, the only clear motivation in one child was jealousy. She did almost nothing unless she felt that some other child might receive something that she failed to receive. Many shy children need to see other children performing before they themselves have the courage to chance certain behaviors. This was not the case with the hostile child described above. Her failure to act was not a sign of a lack of confidence, but a refusal to do anything that might mean capitulation to the adult world. She was impelled to action only when she felt it might mean depriving some other child of a pleasurable experience. Jealousy is, of course, a motive in all children; in this child, however, it seemed to be almost the sole source of any task-directed behavior.

The treatment in each case depended upon finding something that mattered greatly to the child, for only this would lead him to work. The difficulty in achieving this goal is obvious when the major driving forces are negativism and hostility. For example, in the case of the jealous child it meant establishing lessons based on two children, rather than the tutorial setting. Whenever the other child had a demand to meet, the jealous child would immediately try to outmatch her. The policy may seem highly questionable, since it seems to reinforce the child's pathological emotions. The danger was recognized and attempts were made to deal with it by transferring over to a one-to-one setting as soon as possible. Whenever the child showed the slightest glimmering of interest in material or in asserting some positive initiative, this was immediately followed up.

Fortunately, not all cases were this severe. One extremely hyperactive boy, for example, was found to have a great interest in food. In contrast to the frantic rebellion that marked almost all his activities (and nearly drove his regular classroom teacher wild), he was willing to work with reasonable care and attention on any problem which involved food. As a result, all lessons in the early weeks of tutoring (whether story-telling, transformation of matter, construction of materials, etc.) were based on this topic. For example, perceptual sequencing was taught through the use of differently colored candies rather than through buttons. He was willing to work during the entire lesson, as long as he knew that a piece of the food would be his in the end.

Another child had been almost totally mute for the eight months he had been in school. He was capable of speaking, but refused to utter a word to most adult figures. When he did speak, his preliminary gasping for breath made it seem that he was about to collapse. This behavior was so frightening that most adults made no request for him to verbalize anything. They were relieved by his silence, for it restored tranquility. He could not tolerate any degree of frustration, even that resulting from his own actions rather than from demands imposed by adults. For example, if he wanted to throw a ball at a target and missed, he would end up moaning an endless, peculiar squeal. In designing a program for him, the simplest of motor tasks were selected so that there was almost no possibility of failure. Thus, this four-year-old child was given tasks appropriate to a child of about two years, e.g., "pick up the ball," "drop it in the basket," (when he was standing directly over the basket), etc. As indicated by his silence, he focused his greatest resistance in the verbal sphere. Therefore all materials heavily laden with verbal content, such as stories, were held back from him, so that there was less likelihood of his level of resistance being raised. As might be expected, frequent ups and downs occurred in his progress, but ultimately he spoke freely and easily with the tutor.

As is evident in these examples, the teaching was designed to treat the child's specific difficulties. It was an effort that was "played by ear," since there were almost no definite rules that could be established. The guiding principles were similar to those in conditioning therapy (Krasner and Ullmann 1965; Sloan and MacAulay 1968), with the following particular emphases: (1) reducing to as great a degree as possible opportunities to rehearse negative behaviors; (2) reinforcing to as great a degree as possible any behavior that might be channeled for productive purposes; (3) using as rewards any type of material which the child found pleasurable, but which did not lead to destructive behavior. The focus of the tutorial program was therefore greatly changed with these children. This change might lead one to assume that the program was no longer cognitive therapy, but psychotherapy. While this is true to some extent, the cognitive framework was still the vital element. From the start, the basic structure of the daily lessons involved cognitive problems. As the children progressed, the cognitive demands increased until in most cases their lessons barely differed from those given to the other children. It would appear that there are many avenues for helping these children. Cognition appears to be a particularly fruitful one, since it increases the child's mastery over his world. For children whose only tool for dealing with the world has been hostility, the need for such mastery is great. While cognition is not enough, it succeeds in adding a positive and powerful tool to the child's repertoire.

A Representative Interview with a Negative Child

The discussion thus far has been in general terms. In order to illustrate how these principles may apply, a sample dialogue between a teacher and child is presented below. Because the lesson is with a highly disturbed child, it is not intended to represent the format generally used in the tutorial program. It is presented mainly because of its interesting clinical aspects, particularly since so little attention had been paid to the cognitive functioning of such children. Despite his degree of disturbance, the child, James, was in a regular kindergarten program. Upon reading the difficulties he displays in the one-to-one setting, one can project the hardships to both child and teacher of having this child in the group setting.

James was a good-looking, well-built child, which unconsciously led one to expect a high level of competence from him. This expectation made his grimacing, squealing, and rac-

ing about all the more surprising. The ambivalence in his relationships with adults was evident in his willingness to come
to the lessons, but his endless negativism once there. The
initial resistance was so severe that a meaningful lesson could
last no more than three or four minutes.

The interview illustrates the way in which emotional difficulties peculiarly affect the children's cognitive functioning.
For example, while imitation normally represents one of the
simplest demands, and "why" questions the most complex,
James responded as if the reverse were the case. Although he
might imitate people, he would not do so when explicitly
asked to—as though his compliance would represent submis-
sion to authority. "Why" questions, by contrast, represented
a more abstract, unemotional situation which he could respond to with less defensiveness. This is not to say that he
answered "why" questions easily. The situation had to be such
that he was interested, involved, and relatively calm—not a
frequent occurrence. When he was willing to respond, however, objectively more complex situations were often easier for
him than less complex demands. His ceaseless motor activity
afforded the only constant lever for teaching. As long as the
teacher could give commands for action at a pace that was
more rapid than his own spontaneous outbursts, some measure
of control could be exerted.

The lesson below represents an attempt to use a story-telling
situation with James. Meaningful grasp of such heavily verbal
material requires a controlled attention that these children
find difficult to muster. Nevertheless, it is vital that the children develop competence in this sphere, since the skills involved in story listening are basic to many academic tasks. In
spite of its difficulties, it becomes possible to use this type of
material with disruptive children. This is achieved by incor-
porating sufficient motor activity into the lesson so as to both
capitalize on the child's interest in this area and lessen the
strain of attending to weighty verbal content.

The story in the lesson concerns a children's book entitled
Are You My Mother? by P. D. Eastman (1960). It is a story of
a baby bird who is hatched while the mother bird is away

from the nest searching for food. Upon emerging into the world, the baby bird longs for its mother and begins a trek to find her. On the way, he encounters many things and animals, each of which he hopefully asks, "Are you my mother?" As with all good children's tales, the story ends happily with the baby and mother reunited in the nest.

James walked into the room and spontaneously remarked about the tape recorder that was present to record the session. He understood its function, since it had been taught in a previous lesson.

CHILD: Ah—a tape recorder.

TEACHER: (nods) What does it do?

CHILD: It talks and it talks!

TEACHER: You're talking into it right now. Do you want to hear it? Hold on—

While most children would be entranced with this opportunity, it is unclear as to how James will respond with a question that permits him to say "No." (This type of question is offered occasionally in order to judge the child's progress in dealing with a situation that allows a negative response.)

CHILD: No.

His characteristic negative response emerges. While it is possible that this response is a genuine reflection of his desire, the subsequent dialogue does not support this interpretation.

TEACHER: Okay—we don't have to.

Because the point was unimportant to the lesson, the teacher acquiesced readily to the child's decision.

CHILD: *(points to microphone)* I *want* to hear.

This immediate reversal of stated desire indicates that the initial "No" was a sign of resistance. Having failed to provoke the adult, the child tries another tactic.

TEACHER: Okay.

(child then speaks into the microphone and the teacher plays it back for him)

CHILD: *(while the recorder is playing back, child begins to laugh, moves restlessly in seat, makes grimacing faces, and then calls out)* Ooh! Ooh! Hee! Hee!

The reason for his behavior is unclear (perhaps it is embarrassment, fear, etc.). Nevertheless, the behavior must quickly be halted or else it will get out of hand.

TEACHER: *(switches off recorder and brings book forward)* Look at this book—when did you see it before?

The teacher shifts the focus to the lesson proper. Since the book had been used before, the teacher would normally ask "Do you remember seeing this book before?" Because that question lends itself to another "No" response, it is avoided.

CHILD: *(laughs)* You had it.

TEACHER: Right. I read it a long time ago. It says "Are you my mother?" But this isn't your mother, is it? *(pointing to a picture)*

CHILD: (*laughing*) No— My mother tall.

This response is an interesting mixture. The response is controlled and carefully phrased. Nevertheless, the child has focused upon the irrelevant characteristic of height.

TEACHER: What does tall mean?

Even though his response is tangential, the teacher attempts to ascertain accuracy of child's referent.

CHILD: All the way up to the sky! (*points up*)

This response is quite good since synonymous rephrasing is an unusual and difficult achievement for disadvantaged children.

TEACHER: Yes, all the way up there! This mother doesn't go way up like that. But what else? What do you think she is?

CHILD: (*chuckles hysterically*) A bird mother!

TEACHER: (*opens book*) How do you know she's a bird?

CHILD: Because.

TEACHER: What does she have?

CHILD: They have beaks and wings and a egg; a lil egg.

Although he needed some minimal direction, the child shows excellent progress in knowing how to justify his responses (e.g., he can answer a question such as "How do you know?").

TEACHER: That's right. You're a pretty smart fellow! Where is she sitting?

CHILD: On a nest.

TEACHER: On a nest. Absolutely right. Where do we have nests?

CHILD: Up in the tree. (*child draws out word* tree)

TEACHER: That's right. Why do you think they build nests way up in the tree?

CHILD: So, so all the people won't, won't take the eggs and hatch it and, and... (*halts*)

TEACHER: What else? (*softly*)

CHILD: And take the baby bird.

TEACHER: That's absolutely right. We don't want anything to happen to that baby bird. What would happen if they made their nests down on the ground?

CHILD: Oh—Everybody we will kick that egg!

TEACHER: Yes, and if the egg were kicked, what would happen to it?

CHILD: I dunno. And, and, we could pick it up.

TEACHER: Yes—but what could your feet do to it?

This sustained, thoughtful interchange is quite remarkable in a child whose initial verbal IQ on the WISC was 75. In part, his functioning here may reflect his identification with the helpless unprotected bird. Nevertheless, he is dealing with it not in his accustomed, wild manner, but in a controlled, serious effort.

CHILD: Step on it. (in a serious, considered manner)

TEACHER: Step on it—absolutely right.

CHILD: Next time when I walk around and I try to be a egg.

TEACHER: Try to be an egg!

CHILD: No—and I try to get the egg—and then I bring it up here and we hatch it.

The ability to withstand the frustration of not being understood and of being able to correct himself is a new achievement for this child.

TEACHER: Maybe we'll be able to do that someday. In the meantime, look over here, look at this bird's face.

CHILD: (*moves restlessly around in chair —takes the teacher's finger and pushes it away*) Get out of the way! (*indicating that he wants to see the picture*)

A sudden intrusion of an angry note. Nevertheless, he is still work-directed, since the responses occurred in his desire to see the picture which the teacher had requested he look at.

TEACHER: How does she look?

CHILD: Angry! (*chuckles*)

The inappropriate laughing may be a sign of his anxiety at the parent's anger. Because it is not possible to deal with this issue within the tutorial framework (e.g., "Why are you laughing, James?"), the issue is not pursued.

TEACHER: What makes you think she is angry, James? You're right. But what about her face makes you think so?

Many children interpret the request for justification as a sign that they were incorrect. Since the child seems to be getting restless the teacher offers the comment that he is "right" in an effort to lessen such a potential reaction.

CHILD: Because it's all double crossing.

TEACHER: That's right. What part is doing that?

CHILD: (*silent*)

TEACHER: (*points*)
What are these?

CHILD: Eyebrows.
(*whispering*)

TEACHER: Eyebrows!
Right! I'm going to make my eyebrows go like that! (*proceeds to knit her brow*) I'm squeezing my eyebrows together like the bird is doing here (*points to bird*). You do that!

CHILD: (*puts his head on his arms, keeping his face hidden from the teacher*)

This is an example of how the simpler request of imitation can be so vigorously defended against in this type of child. Rather than precipitate further negativism, the request is dropped without comment and the questioning is quickly redirected to a more manageable level.

TEACHER: I know the bird is pretty worried because she has to go and find something for her baby bird to eat. What is she going to look for?

CHILD: A worm! A worm! What goes like this (*very excited—his fingers crawl across page—jumps up, out of seat, runs to door,*

He has answered correctly, but as so often happens, one bit of negative behavior often initiates a cycle of such behavior. It is at this point that the lesson becomes difficult to control. (This contrasts *opens it, looks out-side*)

TEACHER: I'll tell you what! If you want to go down to your room, you can go . . .

with the less disturbed hyperactive child who can easily be brought back with some directed verbal commands.)

This suggestion can be given only if the child *generally* refuses to follow it. If he leaves the room occasionally in this way, it mainly serves as an opportunity for the child to assert himself. If he leaves consistently, it would mean that the teacher has not developed the techniques that permit her to control the lesson. The teacher used this suggestion with James because he generally chooses to stay.

CHILD: (*coming to seat*) No—I was just going to scream out.

A most apt description for the turmoil inside this child. The desire to stay, combined with the refusal to cooperate, is one of the hallmarks of James's ambivalence to adults.

TEACHER: Well, if you are going to stay in the room, you've got to stay here at the table; otherwise you can go. Which way will it be?

It is at this point that the teacher can assert some control because the child has acknowledged his wish to remain.

CHILD: (*hesitating*)

TEACHER: Do you want to go?

CHILD: (*sits down and moves restlessly in chair*) No.

TEACHER: All right then. We were talking about what the mother bird was going to look for. She was going to look for worms. They live down in the ground. You look through the pages and find the picture where she is digging in the ground.

Teacher offers this information (of what food the mother bird was seeking) to reduce difficulty of the task. Whenever a child has encountered frustration (whether emotional or cognitive), the level of the demand is reduced—but the child is never explicitly told that this is taking place. The child's impression is that demands are still being placed upon him, but somehow he feels more comfortable. The motor action (of turning the pages) is then introduced to channel some of the child's restlessness.

CHILD: (*quickly turns pages without any search for the requested item*)

TEACHER: (*takes book; opens to one page*) Is she digging in the ground here?

CHILD: (*shakes head to indicate "No"*)

TEACHER: (*turns another page*) "Here?"

CHILD: No.

TEACHER: You turn the next page.

CHILD: (*turns the page*) There.

TEACHER: Right. It shows her digging away. What does she use to dig with? Do you think she uses a shovel?

CHILD: With her beak?

TEACHER: Right. And there is the worm! Where does this worm live?

CHILD: Under the ground. (*gets down from chair and gets on the floor under the table—makes face with his mouth—clasps his hands over his mouth*) Under the ground.

TEACHER: That's right. Worms live under the ground. But birds usually don't live near the ground. They live in a nest and where is the nest?

CHILD: All (*drawing out the word*) the way up to the trees—to the tip top of the trees (*gestures and rises up*).

The demands are thus still kept quite low to prevent further frustration. The intentionally ludicrous suggestion of a shovel is offered because it often propels the child to offer the correct response.

Rather than battle this primitive behavior, the teacher attempts to overcome it by introducing a concept opposite to the one that provoked it (the mention of "ground" led to the crawling, the mention of "up in the tree" might induce the child to get up since he responds in such a primitive way to his own verbalization).

TEACHER: Very good. Listen, tell me something. How does she go to the worms? How does she move?

CHILD: She flies.

TEACHER: How can she fly?

CHILD: With her wings.

With withdrawn children, it is useful to have them imitate a movement (e.g., pretending to fly) since it allows them to feel mastery in the situation. With a child such as this, this behavior is specifically discouraged since it might well lead to more uncontrolled, scattering of attention.

TEACHER: Right. With her wings. You know a plane has wings, but that's not enough for it to fly. It has to have a pilot to help it fly. Does a bird need a pilot so she can fly?

This is a difficult concept, but it is raised because the child has recovered his equilibrium. The aim is not to have the child understand the structural differences between a plane and a bird (since this is impossible), but to develop a more differentiated awareness of the concept of flying.

CHILD: (chuckling) No.

TEACHER: Why not?

CHILD: Because that is not necessary. She can go by herself.

Again, an unusually well-formulated idea which is so incongruent with the primitive responses that often dominate his behavior.

TEACHER: Now while the mother bird is away looking for

worms, the baby bird
. . .

CHILD: (*interrupting*) All of a sudden it hatches.

The child is obviously intrigued with the idea of hatching, for he has raised it spontaneously at several points. The reason for his interest is undetermined. Nevertheless, it is worth while to reinforce this behavior, since it is rare that his spontaneous behaviors are relevant.

TEACHER: All of a sudden it hatches. Hey, that's a very grown-up word.

CHILD: When the— when it jumps up and down, it hatches!

TEACHER: That's right.

CHILD: Then all the things go down on the floor (*referring to the egg shell*).

TEACHER: You're right! What are these? (*pointing to picture of the pieces of egg shell*)

CHILD: Eggs.

TEACHER: Pieces of the shell of the egg. (*takes another book with pictures of eggs*) Look at this and find me another shell of an egg.

Normally a child would be asked to imitate a new word as a first step in getting him to attend to the concept. Since such imitation is likely to be strongly rejected, it is not demanded. Instead, a receptive language demand is used which requires the child to use the new label.

CHILD: (*points correctly*)

TEACHER: (*puts down second book and returns to the original book*) Now he is out of the shell. How did he get out of it?

CHILD: He just jumped.

TEACHER: (*picks up a real egg and places it in a soft nest of cotton*) Here, let's pretend this is the nest. Now the egg is jumping (*lifts up egg and moves it about*). But it's not breaking. We have to have something hard to break the egg and the bird has it. He's got something very sharp that helps him get out of the egg.

The material is structured to show the child the inadequacy of his response. At this stage, it is essential that the demonstration give an absolutely clear impression to the child of the phenomenon in question. It is for this reason that a thick layer of cotton is used so as to minimize any chance of the shell's cracking by "jumping." In addition, the teacher does the manipulation in this situation since the child may well crack the egg if he handles it. Once the initial demonstration is clear to the child, the material need not be so tightly controlled, for the child will be willing to accept amendments to the basic idea (e.g., the egg when dropped on the floor might break, but then the child can be shown that the cotton and floor differ and that is the factor responsible for the varying consequence).

CHILD: What?

One of James's first signs of genuine interest in grasping information.

TEACHER: You look at his face and see if he has something there that you don't have. Remember, it's very sharp.

CHILD: A little beak.

TEACHER: A little beak. That's the way he cracks it open. You used that very grown-up word "hatch"— what does it mean, "hatch"?

CHILD: To hatch a baby.

The inadequacy of the response is much less significant than the ease with which he attempts to grapple with the difficult problem of definition. This is in sharp contrast to his refusal to imitate a simple word.

TEACHER: You're close. The baby birds do hatch; when they hatch it means they were in the egg and . . .

CHILD: They came out!

TEACHER: Right. Now the baby bird is out. What do you think he is looking for?

CHILD: For his mother.

His correct answers to many of these questions are based on his excellent retention of the story from the first reading.

TEACHER: That's right. Did he ever see her?

CHILD: (*shakes head*)

TEACHER: Why not?

CHILD: Because she went to—to get some food.

TEACHER: And where was the baby bird when she left?

CHILD: In the nest. (*begins to squirm and make faces*)

The restlessness is a sign that the sequence must end quickly because otherwise major disruption is likely again. The teacher, however, wants to have him realize the point of the questioning. Therefore, she quickly leads him to reach a conclusion to the line of inquiry.

TEACHER: That's right. But he couldn't see her even when she was in the nest. Why couldn't he see her? Where was he?

CHILD: In the egg.

TEACHER: Inside the egg. Could he see through the shell of the egg?

This is a difficult question since it involves space perspective (i.e., since he can see the egg and the mother bird together, he may be unable to understand why the baby bird, even though inside the egg, could not do the same thing). Nevertheless, failure on this question is easy to handle through an interesting dramatization (e.g., pretending a large sheet of white paper is the shell and then covering the child's head to show him that one cannot see when a "shell" is around you). Therefore the question, although difficult, is a reasonable one to pose.

CHILD: He could make a little hole.

A beautiful illustration that the child has grasped the central idea without having had to go through a concrete demonstration. The response is also a sign that the child is beginning to be able to defend himself intellectually against "holes" in his thinking. He recognizes that his response must be changed, but he does not fully abandon it. Rather he modifies it sufficiently so that it is consistent with the facts. Such intellectual achievements can be a major aid to this child who formerly regressed to infantile screaming whenever demands were imposed.

TEACHER: That could be one way. But he didn't make the hole while the mother bird was in the nest. He finally made the hole when he was ready to

The teacher consolidates the information, since it would be extremely difficult for the child to deal further with this quite intricate problem.

hatch out—and he came out. And he didn't see his mother, so he went to look for her.

CHILD: I want to sit on the high chair (*pointing to tall chair in corner*).

TAECHER: Okay, James, you can do that now. We didn't finish the story this time, but we'll do it another time.

The teacher decides not to pursue the lesson at this point, since the child has completed several demanding sequences, and his current span of attention is about exhausted. With more motoric material (e.g., making food, building toys, etc.) his attention might have lasted longer. The point of this lesson, however, was specifically to allow him to practice attending to content heavily loaded with verbal material.

The following short sequence is included to show the much greater involvement and motivation that James shows with regard to material which allows greater manipulation. The teacher and the child have just completed cooking some chocolate pudding, and the teacher is asking a question to help the child generalize from the experience.

TEACHER: Let's leave the pudding now so it gets hard. Remember, we cooked the pudding with milk. Can you think of anything else that we could cook?

CHILD: Mm—I don't know.

Even if the "I don't know" is a sign of resistance, it is a much more reasonable controlled response than his former screaming and running away.

TEACHER: How do you like meat? Do you like it cooked or raw?

CHILD: Cooked.

TEACHER: So we need to cook meat.

CHILD: (*interrupting*) You forgot rice.

This may be an association to meat, or eat, rather than to the category of cooking. Nevertheless, the response reflects his active desire to participate in the lesson.

TEACHER: Yes, that's another thing we could cook. So what things did we say?

CHILD: Rice and uh . . .

TEACHER: Rice and what else?

CHILD: Meat.

TEACHER: Perfect.

CHILD: I want to take some pudding back. (*pointing to some of the uncooked pudding in the box*)

This request may reflect genuine interest or it may be an attempt to test the limits of the situation. Since the request is in no way destructive, the teacher readily complies.

TEACHER: Okay, I'll give you some.

Whenever possible, the child's spontaneous comments or ideas

CHILD: Great.

TEACHER: But let's wrap it up so you can take it downstairs. What might happen if we didn't close the package up?

are placed into the tutorial context. Thus, attainment of the pudding is now contingent upon certain cognitive achievements. This is done so that the child will recognize that "anything" can be subjected to thinking and will not attempt to use spontaneous suggestions as a means of getting away from the tutorial demands (i.e., he recognizes that these comments are subject to the same analysis as all other material).

CHILD: Great! I don't know.

The child is excited at the prospect of receiving the pudding, but he has totally failed to heed the question.

TEACHER: (withdraws package so child cannot grab it) If you're going to take it, I don't want anything to happen to it. Do you really want it?

CHILD: (nods head enthusiastically to indicate yes)

This pudding is withdrawn to help the child focus on the question. With the package taken away, the child realizes that its attainment will be achieved only if he deals with the verbal problem. The long term relationship with the tutor has given him sufficient trust, however, to know that the reward will not be withheld if he exerts effort to handle the problem.

TEACHER: Okay. What might happen if we didn't close this and we were walking down the stairs?

CHILD: It would fall out.

TEACHER: That's right. So you think we should leave it open or close it?

CHILD: No.

A typical example of how yes–no choices can cause great difficulty with negative children. They do not listen to the material, but rather use the question as an opportunity to practice their "No" response.

TEACHER: What way could we keep it closed?

The teacher recognized her error and immediately restructured the question to avoid a yes–no choice and at the same time focus the child on the relevant concept.

CHILD: Get a long—long thing.

TEACHER: Like what?

CHILD: That like looks skinny.

Although the child's syntax has regressed, it is actually a sign of progress for he is struggling to express an unclear idea.

TEACHER: A string?

The teacher's knowledge of the content of the child's previous lessons leads her to interpret his verbalization in this way.

CHILD: Yeh. A string. That will be good (*excitedly*).

TEACHER: Okay, go up and look in the drawer there and find a string.

CHILD: (*gets up and looks into drawer, selects string, and brings it back to the table*)

TEACHER: You hold the bag and I'll tie the string (*proceeds to do it*). Is it good?

CHILD: No, it could roll out.

This may again be the child's negativism or it may be an instance of real concern. In any event, he has justified his response in a way that makes it far more than a simple negativistic response.

TEACHER: What do you mean? Show me how it could roll out.

CHILD: (*pulls bag out from the encircling string*)

TEACHER: I guess it could! What do you think might be better?

The lesson at this point could go several ways. For example, it could show the child that the string could be made more secure by being made tighter; alternatively, it could discuss the possibility of using an object other than string. Either course is perfectly feasible.

CHILD: I don't know.

TEACHER: (*takes out a pencil, a roll of tape, and a block*) Which of these might we use?

CHILD: (*selects tape*)

TEACHER: What is this?

CHILD: Tape.

TEACHER: What should we do?

CHILD: Stick it there (*pointing to top of package*).

TEACHER: What will happen if we do that?

CHILD: Then ... it will stick there!

TEACHER: What makes it stick?

CHILD: The scotch tape.

When pressured to justify his response, the young child often adds another label to the object rather than recognize its key features.

TEACHER: Yes, but what about the scotch tape? Why can't I use just a little piece of plain paper? Why should I use this (*pointing to the tape*)?

CHILD: Because it could stick.

TEACHER: Which part of it sticks?

CHILD: (*looks bewildered*)

The confusion is genuine and common. Children are accustomed to think in global properties— "pencils write," "scissors cut," "tape sticks." They are not accustomed to think in terms of analyzing the relevant parts of the total object that carries these functions.

TEACHER: Feel it. Feel this side! (*non-sticky*) Does it feel sticky?

CHILD: (*does so—shakes head no*)

TEACHER: Feel the other side.

CHILD: (*touches the tape*) Sticking.

TEACHER: That's right. This side has sticky stuff on it. Now where are we going to put the tape?

CHILD: (*starts to fold package of pudding*)

TEACHER: What are you doing?

CHILD: I want to fold it.

TEACHER: Okay—but what are you going to do after you fold it?

CHILD: Get a big load of scotch tape and put it all around.

This response may be either expansiveness at his mastery in the situation or exasperation at having to be so explicit. In any event, it is a playful response which shows no signs that the child is frustrated and out of control.

TEACHER: Okay, do it.

CHILD: (*sticks on the tape*)

TEACHER: Why is the scotch tape better than the string?

Normally, the question would first be "Is it better?" Because of the possible "No" answer this question is avoided. (The "No" response is avoided not only to prevent negativism but also because it would necessitate redemonstration of the string and tape and it is too late to do this at this point in the lesson.)

CHILD: Cause it sticks all around.

TEACHER: Right. Now you can go back to your room with the pudding.

Lessons which involved active manipulation (e.g., making pudding) were much easier to conduct than lessons which required attention to verbal material (e.g., stories). This difference might lead one to conclude that stories should have been delayed until James's defensiveness had declined to an almost negligible state. This course of action was considered, but rejected. James initially showed as much defensiveness to lessons involving manipulative materials as he did later to lessons involving stories. Thus, his defensiveness appeared to be a typical reaction to any new situation which demanded control and cooperation. Manipulative material demanded less control and offered greater rewards than did stories. Therefore, it was possible to begin with this situation. The gains made in this setting could then be adapted to the more demanding story situation. The adaptation occurred, however, only when it was demanded by the teacher. The child himself showed little desire to extend his behavior spontaneously to more demanding settings. Therefore, postponement of the stories until James's behavior indicated willingness was deemed unwise, since such willingness was an unlikely prospect. Nevertheless, questions about the validity of this course of action are legitimate. These issues are highly complex and it is impossible to offer definitive answers at this time. The guidelines above are seen as an attempt to specify testable approaches to the handling of these difficult children.

Aside from the complications of dealing with a disturbed child, the interview reflects the type of techniques employed in the tutorial program. Therefore, perhaps the greatest doubts about this approach do not concern its validity but its practicality. The doubt is epitomized in statements such as: "That's fine for a research project. But if a teacher has to watch her every word and gesture, the situation is hopeless. We will never have teachers with this much skill." Unfortunately, there is no easy answer to this problem. The situation is undeniably extremely complex. We know from the many failures of preschool intervention that the problems of the disadvantaged will not yield easily. Even when serious emotional problems are eliminated, the teaching of the disadvantaged child requires a type of care and precision that we are not accustomed to having to provide.

But complexity implies difficulty, not impossibility. We can either continue to develop expensive, wide-range programs in the hope that "of all these good things, something will work," or we can begin to develop education into a serious, detailed science of teaching. The task of reorienting education so that it becomes intricate enough to cope with the problems of the disadvantaged will obviously be long and complex. If the school wishes to pursue the goal of education for the disadvantaged, it must be prepared to cope with this degree of difficulty.

REFERENCES

Bereiter, C., and Engelmann, S. 1966. *Teaching disadvantaged children in the preschool.* Englewood Cliffs, N.J.: Prentice–Hall.

Blank, M. 1970. A methodology for fostering abstract thinking in deprived children. Pp. 1–23 in *Problems in the teaching of young children.* The Ontario Institute for Studies in Education, Monograph Series #9.

————. The wrong response: Is it to be ignored, prevented, or treated? Paper presented at the Conference on Conceptualizations of Preschool Curricula, City University, New York, 1970, in press.

Blank, M., and Solomon, F. 1968. A tutorial language program to develop abstract thinking in socially disadvantaged preschool children. *Child Development* 39: 379–89.

————. 1969. How shall the disadvantaged child be taught? *Child Development* 40: 47–61.

Deutsch, C. P. 1966. Learning in the disadvantaged. In W. Harris (ed.), *Analyses of concept learning.* New York: Academic Press.

Eastman, P. D. 1960. *Are you my mother?* Beginner Books. New York: Random House.

Froebel, F. 1896. *The education of man.* New York: Appleton.

Gahagan, D. M., and Gahagan, G. A. 1971. Talk reform: Explorations in language in the primary school. Primary socialization, language & education. Vol. III. *Sociological Research Unit Monograph.* Series directed by B. Bernstein. London: Routledge & Kegan, Paul, in press.

Hewett, F. M. 1968. *The emotionally disturbed child in the classroom.* Boston: Allyn & Bacon.

Karnes, M. B., Teska, J. A., and Hodgins, A. S. 1970. The effects of four programs of classroom intervention on the intellectual and language development of 4 year old disadvantaged children. *American Journal of Orthopsychiatry* 1: 58–76.

Krasner, L., and Ullmann, L. P. 1965. *Research in behavior modification.* New York: Holt, Rinehart & Winston.

Montessori, M. 1912. *The Montessori method.* New York: F. A. Stokes.

Peter, L. J. 1965. *Prescriptive teaching.* New York: McGraw Hill.

Redl, F. 1957. *Children who hate.* Glencoe, Illinois: Free Press.

Risley, T. R., and Hart, B. 1968. Developing correspondence between the non-verbal and verbal behavior of preschool children. *Journal of Applied Behavior Analysis* 1: 267–81.

Sloan, H. N., Jr., and MacAuley, B. D. 1968. *Operant procedures in remedial speech and language training.* Boston: Houghton Mifflin.

Weikart, D. P., and Weigerink, R., 1968. Initial results of a comparative preschool curriculum project. Paper presented at annual meeting of the American Psychological Association, San Francisco, September 1968.

DISCUSSIONS

HARRY BEILIN
City University of New York/Graduate Center

THE STATUS AND FUTURE OF PRESCHOOL COMPENSATORY EDUCATION

THE MOST DISAPPOINTING FACT to face about preschool compensatory education is its inability to live up to the high expectations set for it.

Most intervention programs share a common diagnosis of the problems and goals of compensatory education. They agree that upon entering school poor minority-group children differ as a group from white middle-class children in the performance of many kinds of intellectual, cognitive, and learning tasks, and that performance differences, instead of diminishing with school experience, increase. The common objective of such programs is to eliminate group difference through cognitive and intellectually oriented education.

The historically innovative features of these programs were twofold. First, they introduced formal and semiformal education to ages well below that at which the average American child starts school. Second, they radically altered the focus of early education from custodial, socialization, and mental health functions to a cognition-enhancing philosophy. Both innovations were resisted. One reason was economic. It was, and to some extent is still, argued that with limited resources a more viable economic strategy would be to improve existing educational resources rather than create a preschool system which requires a greatly expanded investment in facilities and operating costs. The curriculum innovation was resisted by

165

preschool personnel trained in the mental health and socialization traditions. The economic and philosophic resistance was easily overcome, largely because of the impact of the social revolution experienced in the United States in the past ten years. Thus, one of the most ambitious experiments in American education was undertaken with a massive infusion of optimism and money. It failed as a scientific experiment, but the educational and social experiment is not likely to end, even though its pace may slow down. There are many forces acting to foster preschool education, in spite of an inability to achieve the original objectives. Two reasons are particularly compelling. One is that social experiments rarely seem to be affected in a major way by scientific data (see Beilin 1959 for a discussion of one such instance). A second and related point is that such programs fulfill a social need over and above questions of effectiveness and efficiency.

One outcome of the already perceived failure is pessimism about the potentialities for preschool education. Predictably, the same phenomenon will be witnessed in the inevitable failure of "open enrollment" college programs as they are developing in some universities.* Since the data for that educational experiment will be some years in coming we can contemplate

---

* The reasons for the failure will be these: Large numbers of scholastically unprepared students (that is, with reading levels at the 8th grade or lower) will be admitted on the assumption that tutorial programs will increase reading levels and the ability to do advanced mathematics, etc. There is no evidence that tutorial programs can accomplish this and what evidence there is suggests that, except for a small number of students, they cannot. It is argued that moving even a small proportion of disadvantaged students through college would be worth the great cost, which is about double the usual cost per student. This might be so if those who turned out to be unsuccessful were dropped from college. Without dropping unsuccessful students the only recourse is to change the retention standards of the college, that is, change academic standards. In some places, it is politically disastrous to drop large numbers of students on the basis of maintaining standards. The result with reduced standards is inevitable: few disadvantaged students will be able to obtain a decent education in these colleges, large numbers of students will be resentful because the promised results of remediation will not be forthcoming, and the colleges referred to will become remedial institutions rather than serve their intended purpose.

for the present what has gone wrong with the preschool experiment.

As the presentations by the five highly competent and dedicated investigators whose papers appear in this volume show, there is no agreement as to where we now stand or where we are likely to go. Some, like David Weikart, are apparently not prepared to say that compensatory programs have been shown to be unsuccessful, even though they concede that some programs evidently are. Others, like Carl Bereiter, say that while programs on the whole have been unsuccessful some are better than others. Those that are better seem to share particular instructional characteristics. If these presentations are viewed in the context of a number of other program evaluations it is seen that even the best among the innovative programs, although they demonstrate short-term gains in intellective performance, inevitably show the gains to be short-lived and that they do not survive, even with continued educational enrichment. Weikart's data show a typical pattern. Upon entering enrichment programs there is almost immediate improvement in group performance. It manifests itself in intelligence test score gains even within three months of starting a program.

There are a number of potential sources for this surge in scores. One likely explanation is that pre-experimental treatment estimates of the intellectual status of very young children are underestimates. Disadvantaged children, particularly within the three- to five-year age span, are easily distracted and are not good test takers. They also lack knowledge of the tester's instructional vocabulary and have had little experience with the format of the "game" strategy employed in these examinations. A few months of schooling, however, can provide these competencies. Intelligence testing is notoriously invalid under the age of about six or seven. Although intelligence test scores are fairly reliable over short time intervals ($2\frac{1}{2}$ to 3 years), they are not reliable when the child is retested over a longer time period. Intelligence test scores are likely to be even more invalid at that level for disadvantaged children.

A second explanation for the performance surge is the so-called Hawthorne effect. The very fact of being in an experiment tends to energize everyone, teachers and pupils alike. It leads to the mobilization of all resources for learning; gains are quickly made in this state of heightened interest. Habituation inevitably sets in and performance lags unless there is some fundamental change in the system being influenced. Weikart's unit-group teachers whose performance showed the greatest drop (although the others did, too) say openly that they felt they were not important to the experiment. The participation effect was thereby dissipated. Many of the short-term gains reported in intervention and enrichment studies may result from the combination of Hawthorne and habituation effects.

This is not meant to deny that there are gains in cognitive capacity or cognitive performance from preschool experience. It is simply that the gains that are made are not large enough to make up for the differences between the disadvantaged and advantaged groups, nor large enough to overcome the effects of the age-related normal gain that is represented in the IQ score. The IQ, after all, is a ratio score whose baseline performance (the MA) keeps moving up with age. For a disadvantaged child to show improvement in IQ he has to improve his performance *relative* to his age mates, particularly his advantaged age mates, which is not easily done. To expect such improvement is to assume that there is a great deal of potential intellectual capacity which lies waiting to be actualized and that the provision of an enriched environment is sufficient to activate and realize that potential. This has been the basic assumption of most compensatory education programs.

It is an unfortunate fact that very little is known of the control mechanisms that affect the developing cognitive system of the child. Those who support a strong environmentalist position, while not completely routed by the failure of the enrichment experiment, can derive little comfort from it. On the other hand, while the enrichment experiment may be striking and instructive as a social experiment, it is very poor as a scientific experiment. This is because in no case is it possible for experimenters to exercise full control of the crucial variables of the studies (such as subject characteristics, subject selection and retention procedures, and instructional procedures) and thus ensure that study outcomes are clearly and unequivocally tied to experimental manipulations under the investigators' control. Because of this, no nativist can take comfort from the data of the experiments either, since the data are so qualified as to give no support to those who would apply a genetic or nativist interpretation to the failure of enrichment. Interactionists, who probably constitute the majority of social scientists, can also take little comfort from the outcomes, since better results should have been forthcoming even in the conditions of the conducted experiments.

While many practical and theoretical interpretations of why preschool compensatory education has "failed" are available, I believe there is one way of looking at the data which leads to some cautious optimism—that is, if one is willing to accept the fact that the disadvantaged population of children of this country will not be brought to the level of middle-class performance within one school generation, which seems to have been most everyone's expectation.

Whatever the origin of control over cognitive development, it appears that the educational experience provided by the limited school day is not sufficient to overcome either the effects of the child's larger social experience or genic control exercised over the acquisition of intellectual functions. While these conditions apparently hold for the group considered as an abstract totality, they do not hold for a substantial minority of children (possibly 25%) who do profit from such educational experience. Few people seem willing to accept the idea that long-term educational efforts should be concentrated on the minority children who profit from compensatory education. The great danger in the present failure of the enrichment experiment is that the successful group will be neglected through the rejection of the total effort. If 20% to 25% of each generation of minority children could reach a level of intellectual performance equal to that of successful middle-class college students (that is, without changing the present college acceptance and retention standards), then a true social revolution would occur. But it will not occur in one school generation. Those who believe that education efforts *of any kind* will create substantial change in intellectual performance for large proportions of disadvantaged minority students in one generation are engaged in magical thinking.

Whatever the future course of education for minority-group disadvantaged children, it seems assured that preschool compensatory programs will not die, although their goals will become more modest. We may have to live through a few more social experiments, however, before this is achieved. The current enchantment with "performance contracting" and the "open classroom" are cases in point.

If preschool compensatory programs do continue because the social need is great and the apparently unending faith in the power of education lasts, the question arises as to what forms they should take. The participants in this symposium offer a number of alternatives. Most of the alternatives are still within the framework of cognitively oriented training. While Marion Blank's report deals with noncognitive aspects of preschool instruction, the main thrust of her tutorial program is nevertheless cognitive. Todd Risley shares at least one aspect of strategy with the cognitive programs. All such programs define their objectives as providing the child with the resources necessary for success in school. Since the resources that very poor children lack are principally intellectual and cognitive, the training is usually designed to be cognitive and intellectual. Risley employs the same logic, only the resources he defines as necessary for "survival" in the school are not intellectual or cognitive in the usual sense but are associated with what teachers call "classroom management," that is, the maintenance of order, control, etc. The Kansas program is designed to deal with school or classroom management as well as behavior management and is thus more akin to educational engineering and technology than is the case with the other programs.

DIDACTIC INSTRUCTIONAL STRATEGIES

The Bereiter–Engelmann program is distinguished by its single-minded commitment to the use of didactic instructional methods, or to put it in Bereiter's terms, the program has a strong "instructional emphasis." Their program entails "verbal reasoning and problem solving," and training in "the more precise and flexible use of words already known"; it is oriented not to teaching the core content of preschool education (such as every-day concepts) but to teaching "difficult" content (such as reading and arithmetic).

It is ironic, in light of Bereiter's characterization of his program, that he should contrast it with what he identifies as "traditional" programs. The characterization of these other programs as "traditional" is unfortunate in two senses—because of the pejorative connotation of the term, and because of its historical inaccuracy. What in fact is "traditional" in preschool education? What makes Head Start programs traditional? One needs some historical perspective. Although I will not attempt a history of preschool education, some things are fairly clear even from a superficial examination of recent events. Since the 1930s, preschool education (referring to kindergarten, nursery school, and day care) emphasized the salutary effects of early socialization training. This emphasis is mainly on the social and emotional development of the child, achieved through group and individual activity organized around play, "creative" manipulative experiences, and carefully selected materials. It draws its inspiration, in this country at least, from Dewey, the Progressive Education movement, Froebel, Freud, and the Mental Health movement. Teachers' attitudes toward children were profoundly affected by these influences (Beilin 1959), and the philosophy and organization of the preschool was determined accordingly. If anything, this became the "tradition" for American preschool education. In the late 1950s and 1960s with the general "paradigm shift" that occurred from the impact of the writings of Piaget, Montessori, and other cognitive psychologists, the orientation of the preschool was radically altered to concern itself with, if not concentrate upon, concept training. Head Start programs are largely an amalgam of the older socialization-mental health tradition and the newer cognitively oriented education. While a new tradition was thus established, it is less "traditional" than the older concept of preschool education, and percentage-wise constitutes the major portion of existing preschool programs, although not necessarily for the disadvantaged. It is strange that an "instructionally" designed program, which is considered these days both in elementary and secondary education to be quite traditional, should take the stance of being opposed to "traditional" programs such as Head Start. This may simply be a polemical ploy for Bereiter, who probably considers offense to be good defense.

The more fundamental question, however, is whether didactic instructional methods are more effective in teaching disadvantaged learners than any other instructional strategy. There are at least two opposing viewpoints to the one represented by Bereiter. One holds that so-called "discovery" methods are more effective for learning than those concerned with direct instruction. The research literature on the issue is equivocal, giving no advantage to either view, or at best assigning advantages to each in limited contexts. In actuality, however, discovery methods only rarely involve "true discovery." The insights achieved by learners in "discovery" settings are usually arrived at through circumstances that are highly structured; teachers, as a rule, carefully lead children to their "discoveries" (Ausubel 1964; Cronbach 1965). A second source of skepticism about didactic instruction comes from the followers of Piaget. They also hold such methods to be ineffective, or at least less effective than the "constructive" approach considered by Piaget to be more in accord with the way cognitive structures are acquired (that is, through the constructive resolution of cognitive conflicts that arise from contradictory inferences or strategies held by the child). The recent research evidence for this view, although quite interesting (Piaget 1970a; Inhelder & Sinclair 1969), is limited to particular types of cognitive attainment, such as the acquisition of various types of conservation. A larger body of research evidence shows, however, that even the types of cognitive structures to which Piaget refers can be achieved by didactive verbal-instructional procedures, as some of my own research has shown (Beilin 1965, 1971). Although it is not certain that the kind of "true operativity" Piaget conceives of is achieved with these methods, algorithmic instructional techniques nevertheless can actually be more effective in leading to certain kinds of cognitive learning than the training methods utilized by the Piagetians (Beilin 1971). As I will emphasize later in the discussion of Weikart's program, neither Piaget nor the Piagetians offer a curriculum or instructional strategy that parallels their brilliant account of how cognitive functions develop.

Didactic and "instructional" approaches, therefore, cannot be dismissed so easily on either ideological or theoretical grounds, when they can be shown in both controlled laboratory and less-controlled school studies to be equal to or more effective than other methods. It does not follow, of course, that all such methods are effective. Quite the contrary. Some didactic approaches can be quite useless. Verbal labeling procedures that are designed to provide the child with a word for everything in his environment are likely to have little effect upon the child's learning capacity, whereas general rule-learning applied to the logically ordered characteristics of the child's objective reality is more likely to lead to increased cognitive and intellectual adaptiveness and, incidentally, provide a more meaningful context for verbal labeling.

PIAGET AND THE COGNITIVE CURRICULUM

The Weikart and McAfee programs capitalize on the "newer" cognitive emphasis in preschool compensatory education. Both are designed to achieve improved concept acquisition, the generalized effects of which are expected to aid the child to adapt better to the intellectual demands of the school. The Colorado program's origins are eclectic, while the Ypsilanti program, which is also eclectic, characterizes itself as Piagetian in its essential orientation.

Weikart identifies the class of programs, of which his is an instance, as subscribing to specific theoretical goals in which the teacher is an initiator who creates a curriculum in which the child is both an initiator and participant. The curriculum is geared to focus on underlying cognitive processes and to emphasize that learning occurs through the creation of knowledge by direct experience. The child is said to learn through his own actions. While the program is based on "child development principles derived from Piaget's theory," it is also based on methods of "verbal bombardment" and Smilansky's model of sociodramatic play.

Since a great many preschool compensatory programs have introduced Piagetian ideas in one form or another into their curricula, it is worth while to consider the forms these have taken. Piaget, while vitally interested in education, has written relatively little about it (see, for example, Piaget 1970b). His principal educational thesis is generally related to the social objectives of education. He says that if the goal of education is to produce a citizenry who solely receive and transmit the culture, then one requires an educational program in which children are conceived as passive recipients of information given them through the agency of the school. A more desirable objective, he implies, is to produce thinking persons capable of intellectual discovery. In this case one conceives of the child as a cognitively active person who out of his engagement with the world constructs his knowledge of it. The latter notion of the learner is in accord with the Piagetian conception of how the child acquires knowledge of physical and social reality and suggests what the social goal of education should be. To Piaget, an incorrect conception of the child as a passive recipient of information is not likely to lead to curricula that truly foster the child's acquisition of knowledge or to the development of the means for constructing knowledge, although it could lead to the child's acquisition of a considerable number of facts. While Piaget defines a set of admirable social objectives (without denying the value of culture maintenance and transmission), he has offered no instructional model, no curriculum, no educational program by which this goal is to be achieved.

What then have educators taken from Piaget? Some, in theory at least, have adopted his view that education should be oriented to developing the processes and mechanisms of thought rather than to the learning of specific concepts that are the products of thought.* They would emphasize the means, for example, by which the child acquires general classification processes rather than have him learn specific classifications such as those that relate *animals* to *cats* and *dogs*. Most cognitively oriented preschool programs, on the other hand, are based on end-product concept training rather than on instructural strategies designed for general cognitive functioning. They are set more to train for "big-little," "inside-outside," and "up-down" than for systematic classificational or relational thinking. "Sesame Street" is not the only program to stress specific concept learning, although it is certainly the largest and most visible.

Another feature of the Piagetian system that has been adapted more as an attitude than a curriculum strategy is the idea that the child has to be "active" in relation to objects in his environment. This is usually translated into providing the child with a variety of materials that have different properties (hard-soft, etc.) so that he comes to know them through active manipulation. On this score there is also some distortion of Piaget, although he does emphasize an active encounter with the world. The "active" subject-object relation that Piaget has in mind is a very abstract one. He is referring to an epistemological concept—a notion that in the mind of the child there is no "copy" made of the world through passive reception of stimulation, but that instead the child's conception of the world is built through an active construction in the mind. This construction takes place through logical "operations" which are "actions" that occur covertly.

The actions are not external motor activities; rather, they are the mental surrogates for them. In this sense, a child can acquire knowledge of space by observing objects in motion, such as trains or automobiles, without the need to move them himself. The crucial elements are those that engage his atten-

* More precisely, Piaget conceives of two processes in interplay, reflective abstraction, which "furnishes increasingly complex 'materials' for construction," and equilibration mechanisms, which yield internal cognitive structures (Piaget 1970b, p. 62).

tion and create the need for him to think about the external transformations. Piaget says little about how an educational program creates these needs. One can only infer what Piaget intends from the recent traning studies undertaken in Geneva (Piaget 1970a; Inhelder & Sinclair 1969). These studies have been done with the aim of providing additional information concerning the functional relations in particular thought structures, and to delineate further the relation between development and learning. The technique used for promoting the acquisition of logical operations is an extension of the Piagetian "clinical method." It involves a one-to-one relation between teacher and child, with considerable verbal exchange through which the experimenter attempts to create conflict between the ideas the child has about the relations among objects and inferences he draws from the manipulations he sees the experimenter make or those he makes himself. It is the mental activity that occurs in response to the physical or logical contradictions set up for the child that leads to an advance in his thinking. The adroit verbal exchange between teacher and child concerning manipulated object relations provides the key to the instructional method through which the Piagetians achieve planned cognitive change.

This is a far cry from what many educators believe Piaget implies about educational method. It is much more verbal than even the Genevans are willing to concede. It is also more programmed in its objectives than is usually thought, although considerable flexibility exists in the individual exchange. The teacher-experimenter has to retrace steps and try new strategies in the constant quest to understand the *real* question to which the child responds when he answers the experimenter's questions. It is a method that requires considerable knowledge of children's thinking strategies and great skill in working with children. It is almost impossible to use this approach in present-day preschool programs. To my knowledge there are no programs that are Piagetian in the sense I have described, where the one-to-one teacher-child relationship occurs on a regular and systematic basis, if for no other reason than that it is much too expensive in the time it consumes and in the need for well-trained personnel. (Interestingly enough, the experimental program that seems to come closest to utilizing this approach is Marion Blank's tutorial program, even though it is not Piagetian in conception.)

For these reasons a truly Piagetian educational program will not develop with the "clinical method" as presently employed. Group-based approaches that incorporate the principles of "genetic constructivism," or much more sophisticated computer-based instructional programs employing the same strategies, will have to be developed to achieve the Piagetian objectives. To my knowledge this has not as yet been done. As I have already suggested, alternative theoretical and technical approaches attempted by American and Russian psychologists (Beilin 1971) have been successful in creating what superficially appear to be parallel cognitive achievements, but the Genevans have been skeptical as to whether these reflect the achievement of true "operativity." In any case, it appears that the present generation of preschool education programs has adopted a Piagetian attitude and some of its concepts but little of its (implied) technology.

BEHAVIOR MANAGEMENT AND LEARNING TECHNOLOGY

While the emphasis upon cognition, in one form or another, was introduced into compensatory education from the start, the approach represented by the work of Todd Risley and the Kansas group is a more recent development. Its origins are in a behavioristically oriented technology stripped to a minimum of theoretical architecture. Although its rhetoric is purposely outrageous ("survival training," for example), its intent is quite serious. One feature of Risley's program is concerned with managing the settings and conditions of learning. It is essentially environments-engineering, reminiscent of the technology of industrial management. Another feature of the Kansas program is the emphasis on teaching particular skills or subject contents through behavior engineering techniques. The emphasis again is on the management of external factors (through contingent social reinforcement of particular classes of behavior). There is much less concern in this tradition with the nature of the behavioral systems that are acquired. The conception of language and its acquisition, for example, that concerns one aspect of Kansas training reflects views that have been largely discredited by the generative transformational linguists and most developmental psycholinguists (McNeill 1970). Researchers and technologists such as Risley wish to remain neutral with regard to the theoretical arguments that swirl around these developments and to concern themselves instead with the way "activities are organized, how materials are selected and presented, how facilities are designed," etc., and with the development of "new measurement tools" and evaluation techniques. Whether a concern for technology can remain aloof from the conceptual nature of the materials being managed is an open question. An engineer cannot build a bridge unless the design is based on sound physical principles; the same can be said for psychology.

Nevertheless, there can be no quarrel with the desire to improve the management of the conditions for learning. Whatever the curriculum and whatever the goals of instruction, the utility and desirability of maximizing the efficiency of instructional practice and providing an environment that contributes to curricular effectiveness would seem beyond controversy. Yet there are dangers in this approach. The dangers are the usual ones cited—that the means become ends, and in focusing on the means sight is lost of the more significant sources of change, those concerning the conceptual content of the curriculum. It is not uncommon for many of the present class of educational technologists to construct elaborate instructional programs with sophisticated hardware and sophisticated software routines around ready-made archaic curricula. For many technicians the only significant fact is whether the curriculum materials or educational objectives can be subdivided into workable micro-units. An additional danger for behavior modification technology lies in the concern with selected types of behavior, principally those that lend themselves readily to quantification. The inevitable stress is on measurement and less on the nature of the response or the function that it is designed to serve. While the production of compound sentences, to take an example, may in some sense reflect a more sophisticated response than simple sentences, poor quality compounds can demonstrate less sophistication than good quality simple sentences. Thus the more complex construction is not necessarily an indication of superior or advanced linguistic performance. Setting language behavior performance standards that are not related to an adequate theory of language, cognition, or learning may lead to behavior modification that is in no way meaningful or significant. On the other hand, a behavior modification technology that is tied to a meaningful theory can be a powerful educational device. In the theater, a great actor who acts in a great play can create a work of art, while a great actor who acts in a vacuous play at best turns in a great performance. Some people seem to feel that turning in a great performance in education would be achievement enough these days. In the short run it may; in the long run it will not.

MOTIVATIONAL CONDITIONS OF LEARNING

The issues raised by Marion Blank's paper on the emotional, motivational, and personality correlates of learning and instruction are as serious as those associated with cognitive and intellectual development. There can be no denying that learning takes place optimally when the affective state of the child is not extreme in any sense. In most social contexts this is the case. It is unfortunately true, however, that life for the lower-class disadvantaged child, in spite of the efforts by present-day romantics to idealize it, is such that it leads to higher incidences of practically every kind of physical and emotional disorder. In spite of that, the extreme forms of behavior that Marion Blank discusses are still characteristic of only a small proportion of disadvantaged youngsters. A larger problem is nevertheless there. It bears upon the motivational system of the child. Some investigators believe that it is more important to concern oneself with the motivational system of the child than with his cognitive system because dealing with the former will automatically take care of the latter or, more properly, the latter will take care of itself. Unfortunately, there is no strong evidence one way or the other on the issue. Some evidence is purely inferential. For example, the striking fact that there is practically no illiteracy in Japan is more likely associated with the social attitudes toward learning that pervade the Japanese school and family than with the important differences between Japanese spoken and written languages and English.

Less is known about the ways of effecting intellectual change through the manipulation of motivation than there is about the manipulation of the learning situation itself. Some apparently straightforward, common-sense attempts at such change do not seem to work. While almost everyone agrees, for example, that the change in recent years in black children's self-acceptance is most desirable in itself, it has not been the case that preschool compensatory programs for black children run by blacks are more effective than those run by whites (nor do they seem less effective, it should be added). Using the Japanese case as a model, one could infer that the racial characteristics of the teacher are less critical than the learning expectations of the parents and teachers. The social context of expectations represented by the learning goals of teachers and parents and an abstract or analytic attitude in dealing with the world would appear as more likely causes of intellectual achievement.

It is a bitter paradox, nonetheless, that at a time when great effort is expended to provide disadvantaged minority group children with the cognitive and noncognitive resources to "make it" both in school and out, a significant segment of society at the moment is afflicted with an anti-intellectual romanticism that effectively underemphasizes intelligence, achievement, and competence. It is no wonder that a number of minority group members will have nothing to do with *that* revolution. It is not designed for them.

REFERENCES

Ausubel, David P. 1964. Some psychological and educational limitations of learning by discovery. *Arithmetic Teacher* 11: 290–302.

Beilin, Harry. 1959. Teachers' and clinicians' attitudes toward the behavior problems of children. *Child Development* 30: 9–25.

———. 1965. Learning and operational convergence in logical thought development. *Journal of Experimental Child Psychology* 2: 317–39.

———. 1968. A cognitive strategy for curriculum development. Pp. 121–56 in A. Harry Passow (ed.), *Developing programs for the educationally disadvantaged*. New York: Teachers College Press.

———. 1971. The training and acquisition of logical operations. In Myron F. Rosskopf, Leslie P. Steffe, & Stanley Taback (eds.), *Piagetian cognitive-development research and mathematical education*. Washington, D.C.: National Council of Teachers of Mathematics.

Beilin, Harry, and Gotkin, Lassar. 1967. Psychological issues in the development of mathematics curricula for disadvantaged children. Reprinted in A. Harry Passow et al. (eds.), *Education of the disadvantaged*. New York: Holt, Rinehart and Winston.

Cronbach, Lee J. 1965. Current issues in educational psychology. In Lloyd N. Morrisett and John Vinsonhaler (eds.), Mathematical learning. *Monographs of the Society for Research in Child Development* 30(1): 109–25.

Inhelder, Barbel, and Sinclair, Hermina. 1969. Learning cognitive structures. In Paul Mussen, Jonas Longer, and Martin Covington (eds.), *Trends and issues in developmental psychology*. New York: Holt, Rinehart and Winston.

McNeill, David. 1970. The development of language. Pp. 1061–1162, in Paul H. Mussen (ed.), *Carmichael's manual of child psychology* (3rd ed.). New York: Wiley.

Piaget, Jean. 1970a. Piaget's theory. Pp. 703–32 in Paul H. Mussen (ed.), *Carmichael's manual of child psychology* (3rd ed.). Vol. 1. New York: Wiley.

———. 1970b. *The science of education and the psychology of the child*. New York: Irion.

———. 1970c. *Structuralism*. New York: Basic Books.

LOWMAN G. DANIELS
Hyman Blumberg Child Day Care Center
Baltimore, Maryland 21217

VARIABLES THAT MAY BE USEFUL WHEN EVALUATING DAY CARE PROGRAMS FOR PRESCHOOL CHILDREN

SOME PEOPLE in America believe that day care for preschool children is an idea whose time has come as of 1972. Others speak of child day care centers as a political vehicle that could help revolutionize the welfare systems in our country. Also, there are those who believe that "developmental" child day care services can eliminate the need for compensatory education programs for the children of the poor. The most recent advocates say that child day care centers can help liberate the women of America from some of the unjustified burdens of child-rearing.

The need for child day care services began long before 1972, but it is getting greater each year. I have tried to make some inferences as to why this need has become greater by studying statistics published by the Women's Bureau, U.S. Department of Labor, on working women in America. Also, I have read a number of research findings on early childhood education, especially those contained in this book. After my investigation, I came to the following conclusions: First, larger numbers of women with young children are entering the work forces in this country. Second, women are developing new attitudes toward child-rearing. Third, American mothers are beginning to consider day care centers as developmental education centers for preschool children.

Most day care centers in this country today are "service

centers" offering custodial care for children of mothers who need this service. I see nothing wrong with custodial care if it is in the proper context. Bereiter suggests that instruction occurs only incidentally in traditional preschool programs, and the lesser overall amount of teaching is what makes a program have custodial functions. Bereiter is not implying that no instruction occurs in traditional preschool programs, but rather that there is a minimization of teaching. To me, it also means that educational goals which cannot be reached are not set. Bereiter also points out that "The true issue between the traditional approach and the various instructional approaches is not *how* young children should be taught but *whether*. This is still a live issue, far from having been settled by research" (p. 12). The point I am trying to make is that custodial day care programs are not "bad programs" if they are custodial due to a lack of academic teaching behavior. The issue of what makes a day care program "good" or "bad" is the one I turn to now. In the following discussion, a limited number of variables that could be used to help evaluate a day care program will be examined.

Many different labels are being given to day care programs throughout America, and the future will probably bring more. Therefore, it is my contention that the *purpose* for the existence of a day care program and *research findings* in early childhood education should be the most important considerations to keep in mind when evaluating the validity of a preschool program.

Some sponsoring agencies of day care centers are of the profit-base franchise-entrepreneur type; some of these are companies with a "chain" of preschool centers. Others are sponsored, on a nonprofit basis, for mothers who need day care services for their children for various reasons. I have no reservation about a sponsoring agency's making a profit or not making a profit. I only question the ability of a day care program to attain the goals and objectives their programs promise to reach regardless of sponsorship.

Directors of most of the recently established day care centers purport to have theoretical bases for their programs. Usually Piagetian cognitive developmental theory or Skinnerian behavioral theory is claimed. The Gesellian developmental type of theory is not fashionable in the 1970's. Emphasis that was once on personality development, social adjustment, and creativity is now being placed on cognitive development. This sudden switch is upheld by some who argue that affective domain skills cannot be measured accurately.

It appears to me that raising the IQ of preschool children is acceptable if *the chief purpose of the day care program* is to assure scholastic success in regular elementary school. If this is not the primary purpose of a day care program, then cognitive development should not be used as a synonym for raising IQ.

Bereiter believes the Bereiter and Engelmann program has more impact on IQ and achievement than the traditional child-centered approach. He also states: "However impressive the immediate results of preschool compensatory instruction may be, and however much encouragement may be drawn from follow-up achievement data, the fact remains that no preschool program shows any promise of making, by itself, any *permanent* difference in the scholastic success of poor children" (p. 12).

The writer is aware that not all day care programs are or will be for children from poor families. However, one of the major concerns in this country seems to be for more day care centers for children from poor and low income families. Also, another great concern seems to pertain to improving the day care programs. Granted, there is much room for improvement, but most of the research findings at present do not justify strong instructional approaches for preschool children.

Risley has suggested that if the primary purpose of a preschool program is to produce later academic success, the program should be integrated with neighborhood schools; it should emphasize the teaching skills, attitudes, and concepts those schools are prepared to maintain. Wolff (1967) found that some basic attitudes and procedures on the part of the teachers receiving Head Start children in some public school kindergartens could not help but cause a progressive decline in the school achievement of poverty and minority-group children. The findings of Risley and Wolff indicate to me that either most preschool programs or most neighborhood school programs will have to be revised, if the two are going to help children learn.

Researchers working with academic preschool programs seem to agree that structured preschool experiences for disadvantaged children are more effective in producing cognitive gains than programs lacking these characteristics. However, these gains seem to persist only through the third grade. If the purpose of day care programs is to assure the preschoolers academic success throughout school, then I have my doubts that these programs achieve their goal. If, on the other hand, their main purpose is to provide good medical and nutritional care and activities in an "open" framework—i.e., to help the world become better organized for preschoolers, high or low IQ— then I have great hopes for the programs' reaching their goal.

I believe that using *purpose* as a variable for evaluating a day care program will assure the honesty of the criticism. I also believe that researchers in the field of early childhood education should serve on boards, at all levels, that form standards for day care programs. This may help to bring balance and feasibility to the educational standards they may set.

The research findings in this book have several implications that may be helpful when evaluating day care programs. Bereiter makes reference to a common body of cognitive content which seems to be found in preschool programs of all types. He also says that "In the traditional or child-centered approach the teacher's activities may be intended to promote learning of this content, but the teacher is not held responsible for seeing that the learning actually occurs" (p. 6). Based on his own research, Weikart states that "In order to operate an effective preschool, then, the conclusion suggested by the findings of the Curriculum Demonstration Project is that any project must have an effective staff model which provides at least two major elements: planning and supervision" (pp. 55–56).

Bereiter and Weikart seem to agree that the traditional or

child-centered curriculum is acceptable if it incorporates an effective staff model. Blank implies that the traditional group-based nursery school situation is designed to perpetuate the avoidance of learning in those children who have the most difficulty in learning. She suggests a tutorial setting of daily fifteen-minute sessions in a one-to-one setting, pupil and teacher. Blank is the first to admit that "perhaps the greatest doubts about this approach do not concern its validity but its practicality" (p. 159). The implication here for day care programs seems to be not how many people should be on a staff in a day care situation but the recognition of the fact that a tutorial setting is one way of helping preschool children who are experiencing adjustment or learning difficulties.

McAfee's systems approach to the New Nursery School Project could be used to organize the critique of a day care program.

Risley has found that most preschool programs are implicitly or explicitly attempting to innoculate preschool children against failure in regular public schools. Which preschool program will do the best job? He has made two suggestions: First, if the purpose of the preschool program is to produce academic success, then teach "survival training skills." These are "skills" such as sitting quietly, following directions, speaking clearly, pleasing the teacher, appearing attentive, and shunning troublemakers. Three important concepts are "grades," "on time," and "correct." Second, if the purpose of a program is to help preschoolers with their general developmental tasks, then survival training is not as important; social, emotional, and intellectual development are considered more important than good study habits and formal curriculum.

Risley does not make his second suggestion for a preschool program without warning of potential dangers. He adds to his suggestion: "We must empirically examine how activities are organized, how materials are selected and presented, and how facilities are designed, so that children are better served in group-care situations. We must establish new goals relating specifically to living environments and child-rearing practices for groups of children, and we must develop new measurement tools and honestly evaluate all programs according to those goals" (p. 98). Criteria for evaluating a day care program are inherent in Risley's research.

How should we determine the quality of a day care program for preschool children? The answer to this is yet to be found. However, it is my belief that *stated purposes* should be kept uppermost in mind when evaluating a day care program. The purposes should be stated carefully and fully so that they are clear to those responsible for the design, development, facilitation, and evaluation of the program.

Day care programs that are designed to facilitate academic success in regular elementary school may be one way to assure that children of poor or deprived families will reach the academic stream in elementary school compatible with their "true" academic capacity. This may be more utopian than practicable. However, *research findings* should be used as guidelines for assessing the quality of the content of any day care program.

REFERENCE

Wolff, Max. 1967. Is the bridge completed? *Journal of the Association for Childhood Education International* 44: 13–15.

COURTNEY B. CAZDEN
Harvard University
Cambridge, Massachusetts 02138

SOME QUESTIONS FOR RESEARCH
IN EARLY CHILDHOOD EDUCATION

ONE CAN CONSIDER much of educational research in early childhood or beyond as finding answers to questions about the relationships among three variables: the curriculum plan or model, behaviors of teachers and children while the education is taking place (process variables), and measures of child behaviors in situations called tests outside the educational setting (product variables). Relationships among these three can be diagrammed as follows:

Chart 1. Variables in Educational Research

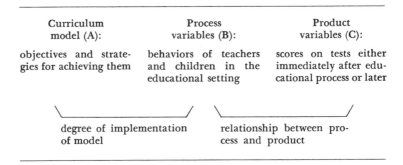

Curriculum model (A):	Process variables (B):	Product variables (C):
objectives and strategies for achieving them	behaviors of teachers and children in the educational setting	scores on tests either immediately after educational process or later

degree of implementation of model — relationship between process and product

After a few comments on where the five authors in this book fit in this scheme, I will discuss each of the three parts of the diagram in more detail, referring both to these five papers and to other related early childhood research.

Bereiter is talking about the A–C relationship, "product-testing" research as he puts it; he raises questions about the kinds of outcome variables used in evaluation (C), and suggests what may be happening (B) in two kinds of educational settings—Montessori and "traditional" classrooms—to explain their lack of effects.

Weikart starts out, like Bereiter, talking about whether preschool education can make a difference (A–C); he then gives a conceptual analysis of different curriculum models (A) and reports his findings that examples of three kinds of curricula have roughly equivalent effects on children (A–C); finally he turns to the planning and supervision necessary to guarantee effective preschools (A–B).

Blank focuses on (B): how teachers can behave in order to adapt a particular curriculum model (A) to children with different characteristics.

McAfee describes the curriculum of the New Nursery School (A) with one example of actual process (B) in how teachers might teach the concept of *un-* as in *untie*, and then analyzes scores on a wide variety of tests (C).

Risley starts out with one kind of model, "survival training" (A), and then shifts away from evaluating preschool education on any product criteria to a concern for what does or should take place in the educational setting itself (B).

Research in early childhood education can, and often does, include variables not included here—organizational variables such as school size or degree of parent participation, and effects on parents or other institutions in the community, such as the public schools. But since the five Blumberg symposium speakers have limited their remarks to the effects of teachers' behavior on participating children, I will too.

CURRICULUM MODELS

Preschool curriculum models have been categorized in many research projects, and comparisons among categorization schemes are interesting. Chart 2 compares three schemes: Weikart's four-way scheme, the three-way scheme used by Stanford Research Associates (1971) in their evaluation of the Head Start planned variations projects, and the continuum suggested by Grannis (1971) for his research on some of the Follow Through planned variations. The extent of agreement among the three schemes is notable. I started out with Grannis's ranking, since that was a completely ordered list, and found I could fit the Weikart and SRI schemes to it by inserting additional models between those mentioned by Grannis. Of the five symposium speakers, Bereiter and Weikart are included by name; Blank would probably fit best in the "open framework," along with Weikart, since his teachers have adapted many of her tutorial strategies for group discussion; McAfee's New Nursery School was the prototype for the Nimnicht model; Risley is harder to place—he uses reinforcement but, unlike Bushnell, seemingly with less stress on preacademic goals.

In addition to the extent of agreement, three points can be made about these schemes. First, these three categorizations, and all others now in the literature, are based on the rhetoric of the curriculum designers, not on what actually goes on in their classrooms. But while Weikart and SRI base their schemes on hypothesized similarities and differences in how teachers and children will behave (process), Grannis bases his ranking on one hypothesized effect on children—their development of autonomy (product).

Second, questions are raised about individual models—particularly Montessori and EDC. Weikart groups Montessori with other child-centered programs "in spite of the odd 'fit.' " Bereiter suggests why, in Karnes's (1969) research, comparative Montessori programs were no more effective than traditional programs on cognitive tests. On the other hand, Montessori programs do fit Weikart's criteria of a strong theoretical model; and Montessori herself supposedly did well with poor children in Italy. On the basis of Montessori theory, Stodolsky and Karlson (n.d.) predicted differential outcomes on a battery of tests and verified their predictions in one school, a nice

Chart 2. Three Categorizations of Early Childhood Curriculum Models

Weikart	SRI (Head Start)	Grannis (Follow Through)
Programmed:	*Preacademic:*	*Autonomy Ranking:*
		1. "traditional" primary grades
Engelmann–Bereiter (or Becker)	Engelmann–Becker	2. Engelmann–Bereiter
	Bushnell (token reinforcement)	3. Bushnell
Glaser–Resnick (individually prescribed instruction —IPI)		4. IPI
Open Framework:		
Gray (DARCEE) Karnes (ameliorative) Sprigle (learning to learn) Weikart (cognitive)	*Cognitive Discovery:* Weikart Gordon (parent education)	
Child Centered:		
Henderson (Tucson) Nimnicht (responsive environment) Spaulding (Durham) Montessori	Henderson Nimnicht	5. Montessori
	Discovery:	
	EDC (British Infant School)	6. EDC
Bank Street "traditional" nursery schools	Bank Street	7. Bank Street
	Head Start Controls	
"Custodial"		

example of model-product (A–C) research. Further empirical studies of Montessori programs are needed.

SRI and Grannis both group the EDC British Infant School model with Bank Street. Weikart does not include it. Where should it fit into his scheme? Chart 1 itself suggests the "Child Centered" category. Yet Bussis and Chittenden (1970), in an independently conceived 2×2 matrix along dimensions comparable to Weikart's, place EDC in what Weikart calls "Open Framework," where both teacher and child are active. Resnick (1971) made systematic observations in one London infant school. Her empirical analysis confirms Bussis and Chittenden's hypothesis, at least for the British schools themselves. Whether that placement would also fit American adaptations remains to be seen. Because of the current interest in "open education" (a category as vague as "traditional"), the Head Start and Follow Through research on this EDC model will be particularly important.

Finally, Chart 2 makes clear one important difference between educational innovation in preschools and in the primary grades. In preschool education, traditional nursery schools are at the "bottom" of the chart, at the child-centered or discovery end. In the primary grades, which includes Follow Through, traditional classrooms are at the "top," or adult-prescribed end. McAfee alludes to this contrast in her comment that: "Concurrent with a trend toward the 'opening up' of all of education in much the same way that preschools have always been, there is a trend toward 'tightening down' in early childhood."

Bereiter questions the entire game of categorizing models by the rhetoric of their designers. Certainly we will be on stronger ground when we can talk about similarities and differences in actual classroom processes and relate differential outcomes to them.

Before leaving the models themselves, we should note that in actual preschool practice explicit statements of objectives are rare. It is a special characteristic of the educational programs designed by psychologists that they are derived from a clear theoretical orientation. We can therefore discuss them in terms of the relationships from left to right in Chart 2. But in most preschools outside these special research settings, adults act with and to children without such conscious thought. In her account of one Head Start program, the Child Development Group of Mississippi, Greenberg (1969) recounts how hard it is for adults without professional training to talk about objectives before they start to teach. This difficulty often extends to professionally trained teachers as well. In such cases, the analysis represented in Chart 2 must start from (B) and work back to (A). Palmer, Cazden, and Glick (1971) emphasize the importance of trying to do this, because an explicit statement of objectives provides the only basis for self-evaluation, as well as evaluation by and for others (parents or funding agency). It may be that lack of clear, theoretically based objectives as a live part of teacher planning is one common bond between the "traditional" programs, preschool *and* primary, which otherwise are at opposite ends of every scale.

PROCESS VARIABLES

Descriptive research on what teachers and children actually do in classrooms may be undertaken for several different reasons. First, implementation of the model must be evaluated. In research such as the Head Start or Follow Through planned variations, where models are being used in sites physically distant from the original curriculum designer, it is obviously important to know the degree of implementation before outcomes are compared. Moreover, difference in "implementability" among the models is itself a dependent variable of considerable practical importance.

Second, what happens in the classroom is important in itself. Sometimes process variables are the primary focus. Bussis and Chittenden suggest that, unlike other models, advocates of the EDC Infant School formulate their objectives in process rather than product terms. In other words, they define particular encounters they want children to have, rather than behavioral outcomes they want children to achieve. See Eisner (1969) for further discussion of what he calls "expressive" objectives.

Even in those programs where objectives are stated in product terms, the experiences that children have in school are important in themselves. All programs should be continuously monitored to assure that high quality care is being given. Risley describes techniques for monitoring children's engagement and their spontaneous speech. Weikart's staff model is the most explicit account of one system for assuring high quality. A critical problem in full-day programs (which were not discussed at this symposium) is the difficulty in scheduling times for staff members to talk together about their work when they are not too worn out from their long working day to do so profitably.

While the procedures for monitoring, or formative evaluation, are often loosely referred to as "quality control," two distinctions should be kept in mind. First, quality control as exercised in business is a negative feedback system whose aim is to conserve some static goal. The thermostat which maintains a stable temperature is a familiar example. Ideally, in education we should seek mechanisms for positive feedback— self-amplifying systems which set in motion chain reactions in which practice and theory spiral toward higher goals and increasingly effective practices. Second, we are talking about increasing quality by attention to the process of education, in sharp contrast to performance contracts which attempt to increase quality by attention only to the product.

A third reason for describing educational processes is that such data are critical for understanding the relationship between what children do and what they learn. Only with such information on process-product relationships can we revise our theories and build more effective curriculum models. Miller and Dyer (1970) include classroom observations by means of video tape and direct coding for this reason.

Compared to the amount of test data available on program outcomes, few good process descriptions are available. Of the five symposium speakers, only Risley provides detailed analysis of classroom behavior. Blank gives actual protocols and has juxtaposed interaction sequences from her program and "traditional" programs in previous articles; but neither she nor anyone else has analyzed her procedures to make such comparisons more exact. Though Weikart does not mention it in this paper, his project has included some process description, such as Seifert's (1969) analysis of classroom interaction.

Two small-scale process-product studies can be cited. Moore (1971) and Smothergill et al. (in press) both focus on teacher-child interaction and its effects on measures of child language development. Moore compared two tutorial treatments over a four-month period. In the "patterning" treatment, adapted from Bereiter–Engelmann, teachers elicited from children particular language forms, such as more extended noun phrases in describing objects—*the bigger blue ball* instead of *that one.* In the "extension" treatment, the teacher responded to children's comments by modeling such elaborated language use herself. By monitoring the treatment sessions, Moore was able to show that in the patterning sessions children really did talk more, and more complexly; in the extension sessions this was true for the teachers. Moore's dependent variables included a range of language measures—general intelligence measured by the WPPSI, grammatical development as measured by a sentence imitation test, and measures of communication effectiveness devised for his research. There were no treatment differences on the imitation test; for the other measures, the patterning program was superior. To analyze further the relationship between behavior in treatments and gains for individual children, Moore did a multiple regression analysis to see how much knowing how his teacher talked and how he talked would add to the prediction of post-test scores for each child. For the WPPSI, pre-test/post-test correlation was so high that there was little room for improved prediction. But for the communication measures such leeway did exist. Here, after pre-test scores were taken into account, adding information about teacher talk contributed nothing; but adding information about how the child himself talked during treatment did. In other words, improved communication ability on Moore's measures depended on what the child himself practiced saying, not on what he had the chance to hear. Miller and Dyer also did a multiple regression analysis, and for the same reason. But their results are more limited because their process variables are available on a classroom unit only and, as they acknowledge, teachers may distribute their attention unequally, and children may get unequal access to particular activities.

The results of Smothergill's research are compatible with Moore's:

Twelve day care children were assigned to each of two teaching styles for 17 20-minute nursery school sessions. One group was taught in an Elaborative style in which teachers gave elaborate task information, and encouraged child comments and involvement. The other group was taught in a non-elaborative style in which teachers gave only necessary task information and did not encourage child involvement. Verbalizations during the teaching sessions, time on task, and problem-solving behavior of the two groups were assessed.

Results indicate that the elaborately taught group gave more task-relevant elaborations and performed better from pre- to post-tests on a verbal similarities task and on a story telling task. The non-elaborative group gave more Spontaneous Directives, many of which were attempts to get teacher help and attention. The groups did not differ significantly on three non-verbal problem-solving tasks or on time spent on teaching activities (Smothergill et al., in press, abstract).

While the two variables of teacher elaboration and teacher elicitation of child elaboration, which Moore deliberately separated, are combined in Smothergill's Elaborative treatment, they were separated in the process-product analysis. Smothergill et al. conclude that "Teacher elicitation is specifically responsible for the greater frequency of Elaborative Statements of Group E [elaboration] subjects since a markedly greater number of teacher-elicited elaborations characterized this group compared with Group NE [non-elaboration] (p < .01), while the number of spontaneous elaborations of the two groups was essentially identical."

Such process-product research is critical for our eventual understanding not only of which models achieve particular outcomes, but why. We also need to add information on child characteristics into our research designs. Bissell (1970) reports replicated evidence of an interaction between curriculum model and the socio-economic status of children: the most structured programs are of greatest benefit to the lowest class children. While this is an important finding, it only points to something worth examining further. We need to know what specific characteristics of the children make them respond in this way. Of the five articles in this book, only Blank deals with differences among children.

PRODUCT VARIABLES

Everyone agrees that we need ways of assessing a wider range of effects of educational environments on children. Additions to the more traditional measures are welcome. McAfee describes a good grammar comprehension test; Miller and Dyer, SRI, Moore, and Smothergill et al. all used more unusual cognitive and noncognitive measures.

It is true, as Bereiter points out, that we don't know what outcomes at the preschool level are related to future success in later school years or beyond. But at some point (unpopular as it may be in this day of cost-benefit analyses), we may have to say that certain outcomes—such as improved communication effectiveness or enhanced self-esteem—are good in themselves, whatever happens later. Some people would extend this argument and say that as long as children exhibit desired behaviors in the classroom itself, we do not need demonstration of transfer, or generalizability, through the use of tests.

Both Bereiter and McAfee refer to two outcomes which are quite different from all the above: improved school attendance in later years, and assignment to "higher" tracks (either classes or groups within classes). Both Bereiter and McAfee report increased attendance for children in their programs, but they differ on group assignment. Bereiter suggests that such assignment may be an intervening variable explaining continued achievement gains both in the Erickson and Weikart studies and seems to deprecate its importance. McAfee, on the other hand, suggests that teachers are not reacting enough to the real differences between New Nursery School children and their controls and implies a generalized low expectation for all Mexican–Americans. In their reanalysis of the Westinghouse Head Start report, Smith and Bissell (1970) agree with Bereiter that improved scores on the Metropolitan Readiness Test could have long-term effects beyond their numerical significance, if they influence the assignment of children toward higher reading groups in school. We need further research on outcomes which can have this kind of multiplier effect, whatever the mechanisms involved.

REFERENCES

Bissell, J. S. 1970. *The cognitive effects of pre-school programs for disadvantaged children*. Unpublished paper, National Institute of Child Health and Human Development, June 1970.

Bussis, A. M., and Chittenden, E. A. 1970. *Analysis of an approach to open education*. Princeton, N.J.: Educational Testing Service, August 1970.

Eisner, E. 1969. Instructional and expressive educational objectives: Their formulation and use in curriculum. In *AERA monograph series on curriculum evaluation*. Vol. 3. *Instructional objectives*. Chicago: Rand McNally.

Grannis, J. C. 1971. Autonomy in learning: An exploration of pupil's and teacher's roles in different classroom environments to develop criteria and procedures for evaluation in Project Follow Through. Excerpt from Second Progress Report. New York: Teachers College, Columbia University, Feb. 10, 1971.

Greenberg, P. 1969. *The devil has slippery shoes: A biased biography of the Child Development Group of Mississippi*. New York: Macmillan.

Karnes, M. B., et al. 1969. *Research and development program on preschool disadvantaged children*. Vols. I, II, III. Washington, D.C.: U.S. Department of Health, Education and Welfare.

Miller, L. B., and Dyer, J. L. 1970. Experimental variation of Head Start curricula: A comparison of current approaches. Annual progress report, OEO research grant CG 8199. Louisville, Kentucky: University of Louisville Child Development Laboratory, May 1970.

Moore, D. 1971. A comparison of two methods of teaching specific language skills to lower-class pre-school children. Doctoral dissertation, Harvard University.

Palmer, F. H., Cazden, C. B., and Glick, J. 1970. Evaluation of day-care centers: Summative and formative. In E. H. Grotberg (ed.), *Day care: Resources for decisions.* U.S. Office of Economic Opportunity, Office of Planning, Research, and Evaluation, 1971. Pp. 442–57.

Resnick, L. 1971. Teacher behavior in an informal British infant school. Paper presented at annual meeting of the American Educational Research Association, New York City, February 1971.

Seifert, K. 1969. Comparison of verbal interaction in two preschool programs. *Young Children* 24: 342–49.

Smith, M. S., and Bissell, J. S. 1970. Report analysis: The impact of Headstart. *Harvard Educational Review* 40: 51–104.

Smothergill, N. L., Olson, F., and Moore, S. G. 1971. The effects of manipulation of teacher communication style in the preschool. *Child Development,* in press.

Stanford Research Institute. 1971. Implementation of planned variation in Headstart: Preliminary evaluations of planned variation in Headstart according to Follow Through approaches (1969–1970). Interim report on Contract HEW–OS–70–134. Menlo Park, California: Author, March 1971.

Stodolsky, S. S., and Karlson, A. L. Differential outcomes of a Montessori curriculum. University of Chicago, mimeographed, n.d.

INDEX OF NAMES

THE JOHNS HOPKINS UNIVERSITY PRESS

Composed in Baskerville text and Bulmer display
by Monotype Composition Company
Printed on 50 lb. Sebago Eggshell
by Universal Lithographers, Inc.
Bound by L. H. Jenkins, Inc.

LC
4055
H9
1971b

Hyman Blumberg
Symposium on
Research in Early
Childhood
Education, 1st,
Johns Hopkins
University, 1971.

Preschool programs

DATE			
OCT 0 8 1990			

27767

© THE BAKER & TAYLOR CO.